Light in a Burning-Glass

Light in a Burning-Glass

A Systematic Presentation
of Austin Farrer's Theology

Robert Boak Slocum

The University of South Carolina Press

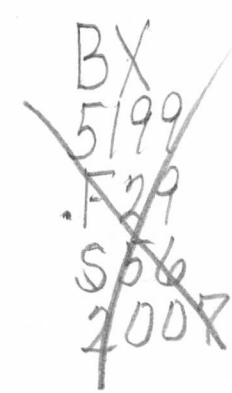

Published by the University of South Carolina Press
Columbia, South Carolina 29208

www.sc.edu/uscpress

Manufactured in the United States of America

16 15 14 13 12 11 10 09 08 07   10 9 8 7 6 5 4 3 2 1

Library of Congress Cataloging-in-Publication Data

Slocum, Robert Boak, 1952–
  Light in a burning-glass : a systematic presentation of Austin Farrer's theology / Robert Boak
Slocum.
      p. cm.
  Includes bibliographical references and index.
  ISBN-13: 978-1-57003-669-9 (cloth : alk. paper)
  ISBN-10: 1-57003-669-1 (cloth : alk. paper)
    1. Farrer, Austin Marsden. I. Farrer, Austin Marsden. II. Title.
  BX5199.F29S56 2007
  230'.3092—dc22   2006026452

Frontispiece. Austin Farrer in 1960. Used with the kind permission of the Trustees of the
K. D. Farrer Trust and with permission of Caroline Farrer and Nick Newton

This book was printed on a Glatfelter recycled paper with 20 percent postconsumer waste content.

Contents

Illustrations

Acknowledgments and Dedication

This book reflects the assistance and encouragement of the many people who made it possible. I want to acknowledge several conversations and presentations that made a difference for me as I worked on this project. In a presentation for the Captured by the Crucified Conference in honor of the Farrer Centenary in November 2004, in Baton Rouge, Louisiana, Ann Loades of the University of Durham, in a passing comment, suggested the topical and thematic approach that I have used to complete this basic introduction to Farrer's thought.

Ed Henderson of Louisiana State University challenged me to prepare a paper on Farrer's eschatology for that same conference (which he organized), and my work for that presentation is now reflected in a chapter of this book. John Barton of Oriel College, Oxford, recalled for me his experiences as a student of Farrer at Oxford and helped me see the living person through his eyes. John Fenton recalled hearing a presentation by Farrer in the 1960s in which he said the theories of the atonement are "more like poetry" than an explanation of how electricity works. The importance of this comment is evident in one chapter in this book, "Poetical Inspiration and Literary Interpretation." I also had a helpful conversation with Margaret Yee, of Nuffield College, Oxford, and conference director for the Farrer Centenary at Oxford, who suggested Farrer's connection to the Scottish philosopher John Macmurray. I appreciated discussions of Farrer with David Brown of the University of Durham and Charles Hefling of Boston College. Phil Rossi of Marquette University suggested Dorothy Emmet as a helpful source on metaphors and analogies.

I greatly appreciate the cooperation of Nick Newton on behalf of the Trustees of the K. D. Farrer Trust. I also want to acknowledge the assistance of Robert Petre, college archivist of Keble College, University of Oxford, and Colin Harris, supervisor, Modern Papers and John Johnson Reading Room ("Room 132"), Department of Special Collections and Western Manuscripts, New Bodleian Library, University of Oxford. Photographs of Farrer were reproduced by the kind permission of the Warden and Fellows of Keble College, Oxford. I am also most thankful for the help of Trish Hayes of the BBC Written Archives Centre and Joan Sommer, interlibrary loan librarian at Raynor Memorial Libraries, Marquette University.

I wish to thank Alex Trkulja, Rose Howarth, and Vivian Alexander for their assistance during my visit to Oxford, and Victoria Charnteski, Barbara Lewczyk, and Ashok Bedi for their encouragement. I must acknowledge the support and wise suggestions of Barry Blose, acquisitions editor at the University of South Carolina Press, throughout the years of researching and writing this book. I also thank Karen Beidel of the press, who has helped to bring this work to completion. Special thanks to Rick Bate, who provided important technical assistance for publication of photographs. Portions of the introductory chapters on Farrer's history and method appeared in my review articles in the *Anglican Theological Review.*

I dedicate this book to the next generation of readers and students who will learn from Farrer, as well as the writers and teachers who will help them. The pages of Farrer's works have much to offer. I dedicate this book to my children, the next generation in my family, Claire, Rebecca, and Jacob. And I dedicate this book to Victoria Charnetski.

Preface

The Challenge and Promise of Farrer

Austin Marsden Farrer (October 1, 1904–December 29, 1968) was the most remarkable theologian writing in English in his era. Rowan Williams, archbishop of Canterbury, said recently that Farrer was "possibly the greatest Anglican mind of the twentieth century."[1] But Farrer has also been described as a "sadly neglected writer,"[2] one who "deserved a wider audience than he received during his lifetime."[3] This neglect may be due in part to the challenges encountered by anyone who seeks to comprehend him. Farrer published not only sermons and spiritual and theological meditations but also works in argumentative philosophy, critical biblical study, and doctrinal theology. He wrote in many genres and forms, including treatises, essays, lectures, replies, and reviews, and covered three theological areas: pastoral, biblical, and philosophical. In a prolific writing career that spanned some thirty-five years, he addressed a variety of audiences and contexts.[4] Few have published so many significant works in so many areas of theological study. Indeed his productive and varied writing career has inspired several bibliographies of his publications.[5]

Farrer's style could be "light, even whimsical," and his learning, which was impressive, was "carried so easily."[6] His sermons were "conversational yet literary, effortlessly delivered yet intricately constructed."[7] He "could be inspirational while possessing a sharp edge," and he took "light things seriously and serious things lightly." As one editor of his works noted, he could be "clever *and* to the point."[8] As a writer, Farrer "had the almost unique distinction among modern theologians of writing brilliant and clear English," and "nobody could pack so much into so few words."[9] Yet Farrer "wrote as a Christian not concerned to reduce Christian theology to what is commonly acceptable."[10] Basil Mitchell of Oriel College, Oxford, noted in an interview that Farrer's thought was "extremely comprehensive," and that in his thought "everything was joined up." In Farrer's sermons, whatever his topic, "there was always a hinterland of thought-out theory brought into it."[11]

Farrer can be fascinating to consider but difficult to master—daunting, even. His biographer, Philip Curtis, states that "when he wrote philosophy he let you off nothing."[12] Farrer demanded much from himself and his readers. He did not hesitate to contend with some of the most difficult questions in theology, and he did not offer easy answers or avoid controversy. He was often original—sometimes unconventional and even surprising. His was a "peculiar combination of traditional convictions with independence of mind."[13]

Who was Farrer? It is my goal to understand Farrer the person as well as Farrer the theologian. When he died, a number of people wrote to his wife, Katharine, to say what Farrer meant to them. These letters provide a number of insights concerning him. Chad Walsh said, "In his presence, words like 'love' and 'God' seemed simple, natural, believable," and that "in the last analysis, it is people like Austin who make me believe that resurrection must be true."[14] Martin W. Jarrett-Kerr, wrote from the monastic Community of the Resurrection to say that "but for Austin I doubt much if I should have ended up here. He had such a way of awakening the slumbering minds & once woken what unpredictables could not happen?" Jarrett-Kerr also noted Farrer's "marvelously fertile insistence that it is the often unpredictable jumps & decisions of the human will that reveal the real nature of freedom."[15] John H. Heidt stated, "This among all his many virtues was perhaps his greatest: that by his own goodness he made all of us much better."[16] These friends and former students were shaped by Farrer, and they remembered him clearly.

But it was Katharine who knew him best and most fully appreciated Farrer's complexity. Around the time of their engagement she wrote him to say, "What a delightfully complex person you are! A different bit of you writes to me every time and I have fun guessing which manifestation it is going to be, and then am Foiled Again because it is either a new one that I didn't know about or an old one that I had forgotten, yet they all fit together like a Chinese puzzle."[17] And in another letter she said, "You are like those Chinese balls within balls; you think each one is the innermost, and the farther in they are hidden the more beautifully carved they are."[18] These letters provide significant clues for understanding the complexity of Farrer as a person and as a theologian.

Farrer does not fit neatly into theological categories or schools of thought, although there are helpful points of comparison. Charles Conti states that the neglect of Farrer "was due (in part) to his intellectual independence," that he was "at odds with the then-current fashions of Form Criticism, Positivism and neo-Orthodoxy," and he was, in any case, "never an easy writer to understand." He was capable of "philosophical leaps" that "could—and often did—leave the reader stranded."[19] At times Farrer presented his positions in the form of written dialogue, and these presentations can be difficult to understand. Regarding *Finite and Infinite,* Farrer's first book, I. M. Crombie states that "it is sometimes essential to know whom he is arguing with, or what distant allusion is being caught up, if one is to get the significance of what he is saying."[20] There is no one theme or principle that neatly organizes the many aspects of Farrer's theology. Scholars have tended to focus on the area of Farrer's work that corresponds to their own training and discipline, leaving his other areas relatively neglected. Such an approach does not comprehend the interplay within and underlying integrity of his entire theological contribution.

This book is an introduction to the study of Farrer's theology in terms of his basic methods and central themes, and it draws upon the various areas of his work in the presentation of each main theme. In some instances, it is possible to discern the underlying connectedness of his many writings. For example, Farrer's philosophical ideas are often at work in sermons, and his pastoral insights are visible in his theological and philosophical arguments.

I have quoted Farrer extensively in this book so that he may speak to the reader in his own words. Paraphrase often falls short of Farrer's originality, and there are times when his theological expression is inseparable from his theological understanding. His work is distinctive for its precise expression, vivid language, penetrating insight, and imaginative clarity. Theology comes alive in his words—words that are transparent to his depth of faith.

This book is certainly not exhaustive in its treatment of Farrer. There is much more to be said concerning him. In Farrer's preface to *The Glass of Vision,* he states that "if we were never to say anything unless we said everything, we should all be best advised to keep our lips sealed." Fortunately, for his task and for mine, he adds that "we are all vain enough to think that if we express within a limited compass what in fact interests us, it may have the luck to interest our indulgent friends."[21] Similarly, if "we were never to say anything unless we said everything" about Farrer, just about everyone would have to be silent about him.

I have expressed within a limited compass the basic aspects of Austin Farrer's theological understandings and methods. I hope this book will introduce a new generation of students to his varied, brilliant, and comprehensive theological legacy, and I hope others will appreciate the beauty of his work and take up the challenge of studying it. Farrer deserves to be heard. And if his work seems challenging, even overwhelming, at times, we may recall Farrer's statement that we are to find the strength of God "by getting beyond our powers and out of our depth."[22] That has been my experience in this and other things. Farrer was willing to take the risk of faith, and he invites us to follow him.

1

Farrer's Background, Method, and Perspective

Austin Farrer, the son of a Baptist minister, was born in Hampstead, London, on October 1, 1904. He was trained at St. Paul's School, London (1917–23), and Balliol College, Oxford (1923–27). At Oxford, Farrer earned first classes in classical honor moderations, *literae humaniores,* and theology, winning a Craven Scholarship in 1925 and the Liddon Studentship in 1927. He was ordained in 1929 as a priest in the Church of England, and he served at All Saints, Dewsbury, until he returned to Oxford in 1931. He lived and served in Oxford for the rest of his life. Farrer was chaplain and tutor at Oxford University's St. Edmund Hall from 1931 to 1935, fellow and chaplain at Trinity College from 1935 until 1960, and warden of Keble College from 1960 until his untimely death in 1968. He was a fellow of the British Academy, an honorary fellow of Trinity College, and a member of the Church of England Liturgical Commission.[1]

Despite the difficulties and challenges associated with the study of Farrer, his work continues to attract scholarly attention. The centenary of his birth was celebrated in 2004 by programs at Oxford and in Baton Rouge, Louisiana. But Farrer's reputation was mixed. As A. N. Wilson observes, Farrer was the "author of incomparably the most interesting theological books ever to come out of the Oxford Theology Faculty," but he was "passed over for professorial chairs over and over again."[2]

Farrer's personality seems to have been as many faceted as his work. He was a man with a family. Philip Curtis notes that his "growing friendship" with Katharine Dorothy Newton was "the most important event of Farrer's years at St

Edmund Hall." Katharine, then "in residence at St Anne's (then the Society of Oxford Home Students)," met Farrer in 1932 in Rickmansworth, where her father, the Reverend F. H. J. Newton, was vicar. Farrer did not propose to Katharine until after she had taken her degree. He was "shy about being seen with her at Rickmansworth or Oxford, resorting to remarkable subterfuges" to keep their meetings secret. They were "like children playing pirates," Katharine recalled. The two were married on April 15, 1937, and they had a daughter, Caroline, in 1939.[3] According to Walter Hooper, Austin and Katharine Farrer "were an extraordinary couple —generous and open and kind to everyone."[4]

Caroline Farrer "did not seem to learn" as she grew out of infancy. Although Farrer and Katharine were "both bookish people," they "had to help Caroline to cultivate goodness and skill in other directions." At the age of eight, Caroline was sent to a special school in Kent, which involved "both a painful separation and a triumphant success." She left the school at eighteen and learned embroidery in a religious community. Her parents had to work hard "to acquire the money for her school fees and to provide for her future." Caroline's situation, Curtis notes, caused Farrer "great anxiety over many years" and motivated him to publish "some of his smaller works."[5] After Caroline went to school, Katharine "found a satisfying outlet in writing," which "helped with the fees" and produced, among other works, three "very successful" detective novels, a "curiously off-beat novel" with religious themes, and a translation of Gabriel Marcel's *Être et Avoir*.[6]

Farrer "was no stranger to suffering in his home life," states Susan Howatch, "for his wife became addicted to alcohol and his only child, Caroline, had learning disabilities."[7] Curtis notes that Katharine had chronic insomnia and became "addicted to alcohol and to the barbiturates prescribed for the insomnia," which led to "unhappy scenes at night destroying the sleep of both." Farrer "feared to leave her alone," and "he would drive enormous distances from outside appointments to be with Katharine at night." The strain, Curtis notes, "increased as time went on."[8] In July 1967, Farrer "collapsed with hypertension" while at the Community of the Resurrection in Mirfield, England, to deliver the addresses for the community retreat. Rather than rest, he "insisted on delivering the addresses."[9]

Farrer died of coronary thrombosis on December 29, 1968, "after months of strain and overwork."[10] About a month before he died, he returned from a visit to Kelham in Nottinghamshire and was so weak that "he had to crawl upstairs on his hands and knees." On the night he died, he went to bed early with an upset stomach. Katharine got up during the night and broke her arm in a fall. She was taken to the Radcliffe Infirmary on the next morning, and Farrer died before her return.[11]

Farrer was described as a "private man," one who "was better in the pulpit than as an after-dinner speaker." He was a person "with the mentality of a philosopher and the spirit of a poet." He could show a "sometimes astringent manner" and "impatience with the platitudinous," but he also had "a great capacity for charity and understanding towards the individual human being and his problems, as well as a wit and humour that had their spring not only in a quick intellect but in a fundamental tolerance and love bred of a deep understanding of human weaknesses." It could well be said of Farrer (as he once said of another clergyman) that "pastoral care and plain friendliness" were "the same thing for him."[12]

But Farrer was driven. He was "an extraordinarily hard and rapid worker" who continued to write even after assuming the administrative burdens of serving as warden of Keble College.[13] Many people assumed that Farrer would be "too unpractical and too shy" to be an effective leader when he was elected warden in 1960, but "such presumption was quickly dispelled" when he proved to be "firm and decisive."[14]

Farrer demanded much of himself and others. He pushed himself and on occasion did things that others did not do. The subwarden of Keble College said that Farrer was sometimes "an impatient and impetuous man" and "could often be seen running instead of walking about the College."[15] Once, Farrer's "lithe figure" was even seen "inspecting the roof of the college."[16] And being driven by Farrer in his car could be a "terrifying experience." When presiding over meetings of the Keble College governing body, "he was always seeking to cut through the knots of debate to get a quick decision—to make time for something else." There were times, the subwarden said, "when we felt as if we were running desperately behind the chariot of Jehu, picking up the bits along the road. But the chariot never came to grief; and, looking back, I think that the exercise did us good."[17]

Farrer's work appears in unexpected places. For example, Susan Howatch uses excerpts from some of his writings to introduce chapters in her popular Starbridge series of novels about the Church of England in the twentieth century.[18] One of her fictional characters even cites his "Oxonian friend Dr. Farrer" as the source of an analogy: God "touching my life in the manner of a potter reshaping the clay on his wheel."[19] In an author's note, Howatch states that Farrer's "reputation remains high and his admirers rate him a religious genius and even a saint."[20] C. S. Lewis, one of Farrer's closest friends, declared that because Farrer "writes with authority, he has no need to shout."[21]

Farrer was "'catholic' in doctrine and 'high church' in style."[22] He has been characterized as "a Prayer-Book Anglican in the Tractarian tradition" and "a quintessential Anglican Catholic"—though one who also believed that "Protestant and Catholic were not fundamentally opposed and that each needed the other."[23] But he "was above all an independent mind, who followed no fashions, who thought and judged for himself, and who expressed the truth as he saw it in an inimitable style which also expressed the man himself."[24]

Farrer's biblical interpretations were original, but that originality has been both appreciated and questioned. For example, E. L. Mascall states in a memoir on Farrer that he had "an imaginative intuition in the interpretation of the Biblical books which seemed at times to border on the extravagant."[25] Charles Hefling notes that Farrer's "writings on the Bible are extraordinary, and they are original in the sense that they are neither derivative nor commonplace. There is nothing else quite like them." But this originality, he points out, can also be a "liability." Farrer's works, often seen as "peculiar," idiosyncratic," and "unorthodox," are not always accepted by the community of New Testament scholars. The "consensus of biblical scholars," Crombie notes, "finds much of Farrer's exegesis altogether too imaginative."[26] In short, Hefling concludes, Farrer "does not fit," although he might be "a voice of sanity crying out in an exegetical wilderness, a prophet without honor among his own professional colleagues."[27]

Farrer's place outside the mainstream of biblical interpretation is evident in a review of his *St. Matthew and St. Mark* by C. K. Barrett, who points to "the large company of the interpreters of Mark who, though they are far from agreeing at all points among themselves, do agree in preferring rational and historical to fantastic criticism and interpretation."[28] Farrer was certainly willing to occupy his own distinctive ground, with or without appreciative support from other biblical scholars.

Hefling identifies the foundation of Farrer's thought and the center of his vision as the mutuality of theology and spirituality.[29] Farrer made connections and perceived relationships between faith and everyday life. His "thought was always tested out in his own actual experience."[30] He was, as Conti states, a philosopher and theologian whose "writings combine, to an unusual degree, the qualities of philosophical sensitivity and penetrating faith."[31]

Farrer "considered himself first and foremost a priest." His chapel services, Hooper notes, "were well-attended, and he had a great influence on the ordinands who came under his influence." He hoped "to retire some day to a country parish."[32] In light of Farrer's synthesis of reflection and Christian faith, the introductory chapters of this book will focus on his theological themes and witness, especially as presented in his sermons, addresses, and devotional writings, which provide an accessible and substantive introduction to his work.

Analogies and Metaphors

The distinctiveness of Farrer's preaching and teaching was ever so much more than mere cleverness or an engaging manner. Even his most apparently casual illustrations invite the listener or reader into the depths of his reflections and are charged with meaning. His use of analogy and metaphor, for example, turn the ordinary in daily life toward moving, thought-provoking, and at times surprising purposes.

Farrer states that "we are condemned to analogize in speaking of God" because God transcends humanity. "We cannot enter into God's way of being and acting: his touch upon us is wholly ineffable unless it moves us to stammer about it in creaturely terms."[33] The problem is that "God alone has access to the life of God in God; his creatures will scarcely claim to know anything of him, but through the part he plays in creaturely existence."[34] But if the mind is "to pass from the notion of the finite to that of the infinite," the finite must "afford analogy to the infinite."[35] In this way we may be led from the known to the less well known or the unknown.

Dorothy Emmet's understanding of religious symbol is consistent with Farrer's use of analogy. For her, religious symbolism "presents an analogue of the transcendent in the forms of the phenomenal, of the infinite in the finite." The religious symbol "must express something positively grasped, a significant relation in experience. And yet it must point not simply to the relation within experience but to something qualitatively other which stands beyond it." It must, in fact, stand in two worlds. And it is this "fundamental dilemma of religious symbolism" that causes "the ambivalent and ambiguous character of religious imagery."[36]

Farrer also recognized the limitations of analogies and metaphors. He states, with humor (as he offers a string of analogies to make a point), that "once the gallop of analogy starts, it is not soon halted."[37] Curtis argues that when Farrer "says we know nothing about God absolutely, we are to take it that our knowledge is never expressible in completely straightforward terms and that one metaphor on its own can and does mislead: analogy is to be corrected and supplemented by analogy and we are the best clue to the nature of God since our experience of God clothes itself in creaturely elements and we have the best knowledge of creaturely existence in ourselves."[38]

At the heart of Farrer's use of analogy and metaphor is the question, how do we know God? Farrer states that "we cannot name him until an analogical act of mind has taken place: it is only in being aware of something finite as an analogy of God that we begin to be aware of God at all."[39] Without discourse on God there can be no "intellectual apprehension" of him, and an apprehension of God is only possible "in proportion as our experience of finite existence affords analogies in terms of which God can be discoursed upon." For example, with respect to eschatology, Farrer notes that "words about our final consummation or true end would bear no sense, unless they bore analogy to present experience."[40] The experiences of everyday life provide a vocabulary and basis for theological understanding.

The problem of knowing God, Farrer states, "is never a problem of his being made present, but always of our being able to apprehend his presence." Human capacity and willingness are the limiting factors in the divine-human relationship. With respect to the question of our receptivity, our ability to receive God, Farrer considers the image of a ray of light and wonders whether God will "pass through us completely, as perpendicular light through a pane of perfect glass, or, to change the metaphor, will he find nothing to illuminate in us, like a ray passing into a hollow sphere lined with velvet black?"[41]

Knowing God requires analogies because "we can only know God in expressing God: and we can express him in no other terms than such as are already significant to us, terms we already have in familiar use." We may know the extraordinary reality of God through the ordinary contexts of life. The resources of our finite experience are the basis for our knowing God, since we can only "actualize an apprehension of God" to the extent that "our experience of finite existence affords analogies in terms of which God can be discoursed upon." As a shadow will be imperceptible until it lands on something, "so perhaps our awareness of the infinite Act depends on the materials for a shadow of him presented by finite existence."[42]

Lived experience—our finite existence—provides analogies and metaphors that suggest theological truths. With these materials we may embody and express our knowing God through analogy. Indeed the mind "cannot become aware of the infinite except by symbolizing it in terms of the finite."[43] Likewise, "all parable draws on the matter of human experience"; otherwise, Farrer notes, "it would signify nothing."[44] Accordingly, "we expect religious mysteries to bear some analogy with natural realities because they are revealed in the stuff of our human experience."[45] If one is touched by divine realities *and* moved to share them with other believers, one "will be obliged to translate them into symbols of common currency."[46] Analogies can help others to understand matters of faith in terms of their own experience, and Farrer was adept at fashioning analogies for spiritual truths.

The breadth of Farrer's analogies can be illustrated by a quick review of several of his sermons. He offers a twofold analogy for the Trinity, noting that "our society with our friends" reflects the "real society" of "real persons" in the life of the Trinity, and that a person's "discourse with himself better represents the oneness of the Trinity: the divine Persons are as close to one another as a man's own thought is to a man; yes, and closer than that." And Farrer provides an application for these analogies, concluding that anyone "who has the character to be either a thinker or a friend lives the Trinity in some fashion, whether he is a Christian or not." He then asks, rhetorically, "Has not God made us all in his own similitude?"[47]

With the image of a magnet and iron filings, Farrer underscores the relational context of religion, which is cohesive for the participants "by the action of their magnet, the life of God, thrust among the iron filings which we individually are, and drawing us into fellowship with eternal love, the communion of the Father and the Son in the Holy Ghost."[48] And he warns that we may be oblivious to God's gift, scarcely regarding "our only treasure, the pearl of great price," which we handle "like postal sorters passing packets and not thinking what they contain."[49]

Another example of Farrer's creative use of analogy is his treatment of death relative to faith. He describes how the sun's parallel rays may pass through the lens of a magnifying glass (a "burning-glass") and be focused to cross in a single point with no magnitude, "which point being passed, they fan out again into a fresh cone. The cone spreads to light, and, were it unbroken by any obstacle, should expand to all infinity." Death, Farrer explains, "is the point of no magnitude into which our being must contract, if it is to expand into the flower of glory."[50] It is through seemingly simple analogies and illustrations such as these—light in a magnifying glass, iron filings moved by a magnet, indifferent postal workers handling packages—that Farrer leads us into the depths of his theological reflections.

Knowing God

God is known through divine actions in the world. His "invisible acts are only known," Farrer explains, "if he reveals them in perceptible effects."[51] We know the infinite in the finite: "God revealed himself in former times, as he does now, by things done on earth."[52] We first know the finite, "and our knowledge of it is the place where we recognize the second fact of infinite being and agency. Remove the knowledge of the finite, and all knowledge of the infinite is removed."[53] When finite objects can be symbols of the infinite, "then the mind's power to know the infinite leaps into actualization, seeing the finite in the infinite, and the infinite in the finite."[54]

Knowing God is not about grasping for abstractions or hypotheticals. Divine action "must be particular" to be real.[55] And "we can think nothing as real," Farrer notes, "about which we can do nothing but think."[56] We may know God as we act in faith. Indeed, Farrer states it is often in the moment of particular action that we "discover for the first time whether we really believe or not something which our mind has formulated and which we have supposed ourselves to believe." For example, he adds wryly, the "man who professed his conviction that the plank would bear [his weight] discovered that he thought otherwise when it was a matter of walking across it." This moment of decision also can foreclose an agnostic suspense of judgment: "The man who suspends belief about the soundness of the plank must in fact either cross it or not cross it; and the act is the expression of practical judgement."[57]

Farrer states that "faith must find an *expression* in some degree of practical trust —in some preparedness to act upon the basis of it—for the understanding and the will cannot be absolutely divorced."[58] We know God through the particulars of our experience and action. In this regard, Farrer echoes Episcopal theologian William Porcher DuBose (1836–1918), who states that "nothing will verify the truth of religion but actual experiment or experience of it. We must live it in order to know it."[59]

God is known through the human experience of God's actions in the world, and "our thought of God is the summary of a tale which narrates the actions of God."[60] Accordingly, Farrer states, "the contemplation of God is dependent upon the experience of his action, however that experience is obtained."[61] In particular, we may know God as we give ourselves to *action,* "in the exercise of a relation with God."[62] The person who stands on the plank expresses belief in the soundness of the plank, and this belief is expressed in terms that are not abstract or hypothetical. And the person on the plank will soon experience the truth of the belief.

Farrer also states that "nothing can give substance to our thought of God but an experience which employs our activity in relation to God, where that activity is something other than thought itself." Will we stand on the plank or not? Of course, the human activity in the divine-human relationship "is passive towards a prior activity of God."[63] God's initiative precedes our action and makes it possible. If we will stand on the plank, it is by the grace of God.

Focus on Salvation

Clearly, for Farrer, God's activity in the world is for the purpose of our salvation. "Christ, the real Son of God, is sent to share our condition, and to share his with us," he explains.[64] We are to know the fulfilment of sharing Christ's life and love, completely and forever. Farrer is not just presenting an intellectual puzzle or an interesting question; he is not merely considering supernatural or metaphysical matters as a subject of academic inquiry or as a way to satisfy curiosity about the divine. He preaches, teaches, and writes about salvation in Christ. Farrer states that "the God whose prior actuality is sufficiently entire to be the genuine first cause and creative origin of a world that need never have been, is equally the God whose independence of being is sufficient for him to draw us out of a perishing world and attach us to his own eternity."[65] God the creator is God the savior.

The process of salvation Farrer describes takes place by God's initiative, not ours. Farrer offers the image of light in a burning-glass to emphasize the role of divine initiative: "The fire is kindled by no business of ours, no preparing or striking of matches on our part, but by sunlight falling through the burning-glass of faith."[66] It is the sunlight of God's grace, received by faith, that initiates the saving process for us—not our feeble efforts, our striking matches. "We come to throw ourselves on grace, but it is by grace that we throw ourselves on grace," he writes. "Before we touch the cross, Christ has shouldered it; before we shape a prayer, Christ has prayed it."[67] We cannot save ourselves, and we are deluded if we imagine that "it is for us, by our own unaided effort, to set our house in order before we venture to entertain our divine guest." On the contrary, it is only through God's wisdom and power that we can put our house in order.[68] The divine gift is ours to receive, but we must receive it, and our willingness to be found by God makes all the difference.

For Christians, "there is no such thing as finding God," but "there is such a thing as being found by God, and there is such a thing as acknowledging that we have been thus found, and picked up, and taken into keeping." We cannot "find" God, but we may lose him. Yet even if this happens, the initiative for our salvation remains with God: "We have not so much to seek about, as to stand still, and let ourselves be overtaken by the swift, determined and accurate search of God." In the Gospel of John, the Pharisee Nicodemus comes "groping" in the dark for God but is encountered by the divine will, "a far more swift, determined and powerful movement" seeking to find him. Accordingly, Nicodemus can only find God "by learning to see and live divinely," and this can only happen by his "yielding to the God who has found *him*."[69]

Farrer emphasizes the divine initiative for human participation in the process of salvation by drawing upon the gospel stories of the visit of the magi and the anointing of Jesus by the woman with the alabaster flask:

> Our incense may rise, like that of the Magi, from unbroken vessels, if we present our bodies a living sacrifice. Yet a living sacrifice is also a sacrifice, and is made so by some participation in the shattering of the vase. Christ, sacrificing himself, joins us with him in sacrificing him; Christ, sacrificing himself, sacrifices us, for he has made us parts of him. We come to offer our homage to Christ, but his star has brought us, and the breaking of his mortal vase has furnished all the perfume of our offering.[70]

Farrer states that we are drawn to the point of self-offering and empowered for self-offering by Christ, whose offering we share, making our offering possible. Christ's initiative and activity in human lives for salvation does not diminish us or reduce the importance of personal choice. God's grace "does not remove our own initiative. Far from it," Farrer states. Instead, the one "who receives the grace of God says: Now I am really myself; now I am caring about what I really care about; now I am making a genuine decision."[71] God's grace completes and does not destroy human identity or capacity. We need God's grace; it inspires our free will. Indeed, Farrer argues that in resurrection, as God "remakes the life of the dead in a new and glorified fashion," God does not force or violate their natures "in thus fulfilling and transforming them."[72]

Human beings are meant for union with God. The human calling is to be divinized and made one with the heart of God.[73] Nothing less will do. Duty given by God and work in God's service are "the means of union with his most glorious life."[74] In communion with Christ, even in this world, "we plant a foot on the risen and spiritual state." Participation in that duty—in Christ—means everything, because as we are incorporate with Christ, "we are not only incorporate with the Son of God, we are incorporate with a man who has reached the goal of creaturely existence."[75] The process of human salvation is fulfilled in Christ and shared through

Christ. Although "the work has been finished in Christ," it is not yet complete in us. "What never ends is our receiving the grace of Christ, our growing up into the image of Christ, until we see the face of Christ."[76]

This process can be disrupted, but at our peril. Alienation from God is "a positive misfunctioning" and "a frustration of our total aim," thwarting the human destiny and purpose of salvation in Christ. Indeed, "if we are not reconciled to God," Farrer warns, "we are spoiling the music, we are not just letting the music alone."[77]

Pastoral and Ethical Applications

Farrer's theology does not end in abstract hypotheticals or speculation. It leads to a real expression of faith in terms of the believer's circumstances in the world. Our duty in life, given to us by God, "is the means of union with his most glorious life." The Christian is to find "delight" in God and not be "a reluctant, slavish worker in his service."[78] Indeed, Farrer states that "the new miracle of Christ's religion is the union of duty with delight."[79] To pursue a calling that is worth pursuing will make for happiness that is "entire."[80]

Faith calls for a lived expression, an ethic for Christian living that faces up to the real problems Christians encounter in life. Human actions—not words alone, not feelings alone—evidence desire for God. "Nothing but action," Farrer states, "can give seriousness to our desire for God."[81] At the heart of our Christian lives is God's mercy and compassion. Poverty, mourning, and hunger, "when combined with faith," serve to throw us on the compassion of God.[82] Farrer's understanding may be compared to that of DuBose, who states, "Our Lord makes poverty the first condition of spiritual blessedness, because in it begins all that dependence upon God the end of which is oneness with Him. Out of that poverty come all godly sorrow, all noble meekness and humility, all hunger and thirst for rightness and fullness of life, all faith in God, all hope in self, all true self-realization and soul satisfaction."[83]

It is God's mercy and not *our rights* that we need, Farrer urges, and this understanding, this realization, says much about how we are to live. "Having rights is damnation," he states, and "perhaps hell is for those who ask for it." In demanding our rights, we may get what we deserve (which can be a frightening prospect), but as we rely on divine help instead of asserting our rights, we may know God's compassion and be engaged not in terms of our merits "but in accordance with his mercy."[84]

Spiritual Integrity

For Farrer, the "whole issue in the religious life" is "not to be a double thinker, or any how, to be less and less of one."[85] His treatment of the problem recalls Augustine's dilemma as he approached conversion. In his *Confessions,* Augustine described a "morbid condition of the mind which, when it is lifted up by the truth, does not unreservedly rise to it but is weighed down by habit. So there are two wills." He recalled that "in my own case, as I deliberated about serving my Lord God (Jer. 30:9) which I had long been disposed to do, the self which willed to serve was identical with the self which was unwilling. . . . I was neither wholly willing nor wholly unwilling. So I was in conflict with myself and was dissociated from myself."[86]

Farrer recognizes the serious threat of double-mindedness for a Christian. When Christianity is taken seriously, double thinking is no mere "amiable and harmless hypocrisy." Indeed, Farrer states, "Christian hypocrisy is not amiable or harmless at all." All are sinners and are inevitably tarred with the brush of hypocrisy, but all can be saved from that hypocrisy by faith. As we live our lives, God "is forcing the two parts of our thinking together."[87] Farrer emphasizes the importance of Christian authenticity, which, with the grace of God, allows the diverging and inconsistent aspects of a life to be drawn into a unified and faithful whole.

Humility and Sacrifice

Farrer clearly identifies the place of humility and sacrifice in living Christian faith. Jesus is the prime example, and he reveals the striking contrasts of the Christian life. Farrer notes that "the maker of the world is born a begging child; he begs for milk, and does not know that it is milk for which he begs."[88] We know Jesus in weakness, from the vulnerability of a humble birth to the vulnerability of death on a cross, "naked on the wood."[89] And yet "the weakness of God proves stronger than men, and the folly of God proves wiser than men." God's love is "the strongest instrument of omnipotence" for accomplishing the divine purposes on earth, and God's love is brought to bear on human pride "by weakness not by strength, by need and not by bounty."[90] God's ultimate power and God's love are made known in Jesus's vulnerability.

We know Christ through "two sorts of deputies in the world, two sorts of human substitutes for himself." The "deputies of his power" are Christ's apostolic ministers, who speak his word, pronounce his pardon, and "give his body and blood," but the "deputies of his weakness are the little and the needy."[91] By Christ's inspiration, Farrer states, "we will receive Christ in both sorts of his human deputies, but more endearing, more revealing, more present to us at all times, are the deputies of his weakness." Through them, "his infant hands receive our Christmas gifts, and his gratitude, unlike ours, is undying."[92] In this regard, Farrer recalls Jesus's statement (Matt. 18:5) that whoever welcomes a humble child in Jesus's name welcomes Jesus.[93] We find Christ and serve him as we care for the needy and humble in the world.

It is "Christ's revelation of redemptive suffering, and everlasting life" that "interprets to us the action of God's mysterious hands."[94] Christ provides an example of loving humility. As we accept the reality of who Christ is and what he offers, we must face our limitations and dependence on God. It is Jesus's suffering and death—not our own—that is "the way back from sin to freedom." Therefore we must accept daily the "infinite generosity" of Christ and acknowledge our "impotence to atone."[95] Christ's life also provides a clear invitation for those who would follow. As Jesus, who is known in his humility and sacrifice, "does not stand on his own dignity," it is likewise "a small thing that we should endure being fools for Christ's sake." As Christians following Christ, "we must put up with such humiliation of ourselves," Farrer states, "or better still, forget ourselves altogether."[96] Christian faith points us beyond ourselves.

We must have the humility to center our trust in God, not in ourselves, Farrer states. He warns that "those who lift themselves up, or are exalted by any hand other than the divine, get above themselves and are ripe for a fall." In contrast, God lifts up "those who deflate themselves of all pretension and sink to the level of their true condition." As in Christ's own ascension, God lifts up the abased and "sets them on high," giving them glory and power and bringing them "near to himself, in the high and holy place where he dwells."[97] If we "think we can trust ourselves to be faithful to God," we will "lose heart in religion," break down, and become discouraged. Faith must not be self-centered. Religion is "trust in the faithfulness of God," not "pretending to be faithful." Christians need the humility to rely on God's help, and in that humility, they may return to God "again and again and again for forgiveness and a fresh start."[98]

Farrer emphasized the need for humility relative to the Christian priesthood in an ordination sermon preached in 1961. Speaking on behalf of priests, he said that "the obstacles we may put in the way of the gospel may be endless; but endless also the graces which Christ may, and indeed will, give to others over our shoulders and from behind our backs." There is an inevitable "gulf" between what the priest is and what the priest represents, "which the Christian priest can neither acquiesce in, nor bridge over." The priest, he said, "can only be amazed at what God has done through him for the blessing of others, in spite of what he knows himself to be."[99] Ordained ministry is possible as God works through the life and limitations of the priest.

Humility has everything to do with facing our limitations and failures and finding God's presence in the midst of our shortcomings. In that sense, our failures and shortcomings are a critical part of the Christian life. "Happy is the man who learns from his own failures," Farrer states. "He certainly won't learn from anyone else's."[100] He also notes that "we do not learn what dependence on God is, except through having our self-dependence broken in the mill of life, slowly and painfully." This breaking of self-dependence is an experience of the cross, which all Christians must share. For "those who pledge themselves to God," Farrer warns, there will be "many tears, much shame, continual repentance."[101]

Farrer states that when we fall short of the glory of God, at least we are in good company.[102] He notes that "S. Mark (if he is indeed the same man) went back from the work in Pamphylia, and in Gethsemane none of the disciples behaved with credit." Jesus's closest followers were no strangers to failure. And yet, Farrer advises, "it is by these desolating experiences that God teaches us to trust him, not ourselves. The more emptied out you are, the more hope there is of your learning to be a Christian."[103] Episcopal priest and author Alan Jones quotes a Tibetan saying: "The crack in the heart lets the mystery in."[104] In other words, our moments of pain and loss may provide the occasion for knowing God more fully.

Face to face with our limitations and failures, we may begin to trust God. This means letting go of illusions of self-sufficiency and acknowledging our dependence upon God. As Farrer states in another context, "We must abandon ourselves to the will of Christ if we are to be his disciples."[105] Ultimately it means our death —the death of our false and self-centered self, the death of everything in us that thwarts God's activity, the death of even our mortal selves, if "we die so that everything we have become in our living is handed back to the God who gave us life for him to refashion and use according to his pleasure." In this sense, "in the eyes of God our dying is not simply negative, it is an immensely important and salutary thing" because "by dying we become God's."[106] By sacrifice, humility, and self-abandonment, it is possible to fulfill our life as God's own.

A Man of Prayer

Farrer was first and foremost a man of prayer. His love for God was expressed in what he did and said, and he hoped to share with others his relationship with God. The theological fine points in his works are never for their own sake. For Farrer, "prayer and dogma are inseparable," and "either without the other is meaningless and dead." True dogmas must be prayable, and true Christians must pray them.[107] The Christian faith is to be both understood and lived.

Farrer encourages all kinds of prayers. He emphasizes the importance of regular participation in the Eucharist (sometimes known as Holy Communion), asking his hearers, "Don't you know that Christ wants you there, that he has died to give you what you there receive, at what is the weekly resurrection of the body of Christ?"[108] He responds with scorn to the suggestion that familiarity breeds contempt in terms of receiving the Eucharist[109] and urges the tradition of "a thousand years and half a thousand more" that a Christian choosing to be absent from the Sunday Eucharist without being physically prevented "would be guilty of maiming the physical body of Christ."[110]

With respect to prayer, as with all of life, our receiving the generous outpouring of divine love is to lead to right actions and concern for others in the world. Farrer notes that praying for others "is not something different from bringing yourself before God." As we pray, he advises, "the more you look outwards, the more you will be yourself."[111] Prayer is no mere abstraction. Instead, prayer "that does not issue in practical resolutions is a delusion,"[112] and "if prayer issues in no resolutions, and if no resolutions are ever kept, little will happen towards our sanctification."[113]

True prayer leads us beyond ourselves. We literally *cannot* pray for the effects of God's love in our own lives while rejecting the effects of God's love through us on others. "That prayer is unprayable," Farrer states. Similarly we cannot ask for God's compassion on us, just as we are, "without one plea," while rejecting others, "just as they are, not with any number of pleas." If we apply such a double standard, "the whole channel of our communication with our creator is blocked," so that our prayers cannot "find heaven" and God's grace cannot descend on us.[114] In this regard, Farrer's understanding recalls the words of the Lord's Prayer: "Forgive us our debts, as we also have forgiven our debtors."[115] Forgiveness and mercy may be envisioned as a door that must be open *from* us in order to be open *to* us.

Farrer asserts that we are not just to pray for what we want, offering a kind of heavenly wish list. As we pray in ways that may be difficult for us, we may discover God transforming us in surprising ways. Farrer explains how we may experience the "fruits of grace" in prayer: "We pray for those whom we dislike, and care for them; we pray to do the duties we detest, and delight in them."[116] Prayer can change us, Farrer notes, and we should not be reluctant to pray an "insincere prayer until he who is sincerity and truth itself overcomes" us. We should pray until our prayers cease to be ours alone and we are warmed into life by "the sun of God's charity." Indeed we can pray ourselves "out of prayerlessness."[117]

We may know God, and we are meant to know God—especially in prayer. "We know, on our knees, and in the depth of our heart, what Christ is, by knowing what he has made us," Farrer states, "and we know what he has made us, by knowing what he is."[118] For Farrer, knowing is praying. The life of prayer is our primary epistemology. As we pray, we may become aware that we are called to more than an abstract sense of duty. Our faith is to be lived. The "secret of life" is that "we know our lives in terms of God," and that knowledge distinguishes the Christian from the "serious atheist." Therefore, "it is infinitely worthwhile to pray, if only to realise that in all our life it is God's will with which we have to do."[119]

Our prayer is life, as we share God's life in prayer. Farrer explains that "God's presence, spirit, power and love" are poured into our church, our bodies, and our souls "like wine into cups, as much as they will contain, and then overflow." With respect to God's generous outpouring of love, Farrer promises that "all the room you give him, he will fill."[120] And so we are to "abide" in God, "springing" back to God again and again, with "a certain elasticity."[121] Farrer's metaphors and analogies are wonderfully mixed throughout his work, but his message is altogether clear: we are to live in prayer, and know the love of God, and care for others generously.

2

Farrer's Systematic Themes

Although Farrer's work, taken as a whole, is a comprehensive theological contribution, he did not write or present it systematically. It is possible to identify and make explicit the various areas of his theology as points of reference for understanding his work, but this can be a challenging exercise, because one area of thought often leads seamlessly into another. Yet it is possible to trace threads of connection in Farrer's work and thereby understand the interrelatedness of his various writings.

Humanity (Theological Anthropology)

Because Farrer's analogies begin with human experience, his understanding of human nature provides an appropriate starting point for considering his theology in a systematic way. It is only in our lives as human beings that "we can possibly touch the nerve of God's creative action, or experience creation taking place."[1] The human being is Farrer's "specimen creature," so that the "nerve of existence, or the quality of life" in itself gives him "a clue" about "other existences by whatsoever analogy they bear to my own."[2] He starts with the person, "the willing I, the I who chooses and cares," who is "that real I which has to meet God's will." This is the most basic "point of contact: I have to face God."[3] Farrer likewise states that it is necessarily "through an extension of our self-understanding" that we consider "the being of all things."[4]

A freely chosen engagement in the saving process is necessary—and indeed called for from a divine perspective. God never reduces us to robots or puppets, not even for the sake of our salvation. "God's plans," Farrer states, "do not simply leave room for free operators, they employ free operators in carrying them out."[5]

And yet our free will may not be all that we think it is. Drawing on a psychological understanding of the human unconscious, Farrer warns that "our independent freedom of will is very slight: it is the conscious surface of the mind." There are "depths beneath, of which we have little notion, and which, doubtless, affect our actions to an indeterminable extent."[6] Farrer uses the analogy of himself swimming over deep water to illustrate this understanding of our "conscious life," observing:

> We keep to the surface of our mind and think we are free. We make a great to-do with our kicking and striking, and think that we are going where we choose; but when we look round and take our bearings, we find it is the currents that have carried us.[7]

We do have free will, and it matters greatly, but we may also be "moved" by influences that affect us below and beyond the level of conscious decision.

Farrer also considers the basis of our humanity in terms of how we come to full personhood. The first answer would be: *not by ourselves*. "To some considerable extent," Farrer states, "we all owe what we are to the free efforts of others, say of our parents."[8] He uses the "tale" of human children raised by a she-wolf to illustrate our need for other human beings to assist in our own emerging personhood. "If we could have been brought up by wolves," Farrer notes, "they could have made nothing better than wolves of us." We would have remained "like idiots in the cradle" if "no one had smiled us into smiling back, or talked us into talking."[9] In short, he states, "mentality as we know it is a social product" and "thought is the interiorisation of dialogue."[10] Even our interior processes of thought have been formed through interactions with others and would be diminished without others.

The process of humanizing children through relationship also can be seen relative to faith. Farrer states that children "are born potentially human, that is all." They "are smiled and talked into being actually so." Likewise, children are "talked and loved into religious belief."[11] Farrer explains that "from first infancy our elders loved us, played us, served us, talked us into knowing them; and so the believer claims that he has been brought by mediated divine initiatives into the knowledge of God."[12] It is God's loving initiative that draws us into the divine-human relationship. Our knowing God is relational, prompted by God's invitation.

Our humanizing through relationship calls for more than other persons. We need God. Drawing on the story of King Nebuchadnezzar in chapter 4 of the book of Daniel, Farrer states that we can only hold on to our humanity "by attachment to deity." In his arrogance, Nebuchadnezzar loses "his hold on heaven" and consequently "grovels to the earth."[13] Humanity cut off from God becomes something less than true humanity. Nebuchadnezzar, guilty of setting up his own God, became a beast. His story is a parable of the empires and cultures that "find it easy to deify themselves, because the gods they worship are no higher than their own heads." As human beings, we are animals, but we are more than animals, as we have "breathed a breath of the divine Spirit," and we may live "by coming up to breathe, like a diver—to breathe the air of the divine kingdom."[14] In short, states Farrer, we need the presence of divinity in our lives, we need the breath of God for the fullness of our humanity.

The Christ (Christology)

Farrer's approach to anthropology carries over into his christology as he emphasizes the realities of human experience as a starting point for understanding.[15] In Christ the human story "loses all its opaqueness" as the natural medium for divine action.[16] Christ incarnates true humanity. Farrer states that "Christ recovers to man his true nature, and the recovery of that nature is the recovery of knowledge—knowledge of God, and knowledge of ourselves. If the likeness of God is straightened out in us again, it shows us both what God is, and what he intends us to do in imitation of him, within the assigned limits of our being."[17]

Jesus lived a human life: he was born to a human mother, he grew up, he had relationships with others, he made decisions and acted in specific ways, and he died. Jesus would not have been human if he had been exempted from the pain and limitations of the human condition. "Christ is very God, indeed," Farrer notes, "but also very man; and an omniscient being who knows all the answers before he thinks and all the future before he acts is not a man at all, he has escaped the human predicament."[18]

Jesus was not "a divinely mesmerized sleepwalker, a jointed doll pulled by heavenly wires," or "a painful pedant, carrying out with pharisaic exactitude a part which had been written for him by a divine hand."[19] Jesus had nothing less than a full humanity, and his humanity was lived in ways that we can understand. Indeed we must understand Jesus's humanity to understand him.

Farrer offers an interesting analogy to bring home the reality of Jesus's necessary human growth and development. Noting that Jesus "learnt the job of living in the school of life," Farrer states that Jesus "had no bad carpentry to unlearn, when he learnt his carpentry from Joseph; he had to learn it, just the same, by mastering in order the tasks his earthly father set him." Similarly, Jesus "had virtue, or obedience, to learn from his heavenly Father, by rightly deciding every choice which Providence presented to him."[20] These were human decisions and situations that Jesus encountered humanly.

Jesus was one with the Holy Spirit, but "no Christian will suppose for a moment that Jesus in his carpentry shop ever laid aside the hammer and used the Holy Ghost to drive an awkward nail."[21] Jesus lived humanly. He had to grow up. And like us, he encountered the challenges, opportunities, and frustrations of life through his own human actions and decisions. Yet it is important to realize that for all Farrer's carpentry imagery, for all the reality of Jesus's humanity and despite the realization that "everything Jesus does is human and natural, and the speech or act of a Galilean carpenter," Farrer is entirely clear that God speaks through Jesus's "perfect human nature."[22]

Jesus was not "a god in masquerade" in a docetic sense of merely seeming to be human. His humanity was "as entire as his deity," and he "spared himself nothing" of human experience. Jesus "wove up his life, as each of us must, out of the materials that were to hand. He found his way by groping and he knew his Father by trusting; only he made no false moves."[23] Although Jesus lived without sin, he did not walk "down from heaven a readymade man, with a complete outfit of true ideas in his head." Instead, "he needed a mother to smile at him, a father to talk to him, if he was ever going to be a man." He needed his parents, kindred, and friends—as do we all, because "we cannot go on being human, anymore than we can get to be human, without other people."[24] Jesus lived the process of human growth and development, and he needed others as he grew to be the person he became.

Jesus did not become Jesus or live as Jesus in isolation from others. For him, as for us, "humanity is a social fact."[25] Jesus's very identity was shaped by Mary and Joseph, by the unknown rabbi of his village, by "the disciples to whom he gave himself and the poor people to whose need he ministered," so that "the life of God, incarnate in Jesus," was in fact "a spreading complex of personal being, centred in Jesus, and annexing his companions." Indeed, all the faithful are included in "the social body of Christ," and "he is what he humanly is by his relation to us."[26] Jesus's humanity was a social reality, as is our humanity for all of us.

Of particular interest to Farrer was Jesus's human struggle with the meaning of his life and vocation as Son of God. He was, of course, "the Son of God from all eternity," so there was no question of him needing to "become the divine Son of God" in an adoptionistic sense. Nothing ever needed to be added to Jesus's divinity. And yet Jesus "had to realize and to live out what he was in terms of human life," and that was a human realization he could not have achieved when he was in the cradle.[27] It was necessary for Jesus to grow into a human realization of who he was and what his life should be.

The particular difficulty for Jesus's human understanding of his identity was that "he was called upon to be the Son of God in the world, when it was still unknown what it meant to be that." There were no human role models for Jesus's life as the Son of God. But Christians now have Jesus's example of human righteousness. Farrer states that we "have far clearer waymarks on the road we are to tread; we have all the beacons he lighted and left us in his passage through the world."[28] Of course, we need not assume that Jesus "started from the point which the faith of the Church ultimately reached." Instead, "he would more naturally begin by deepening the messianic hopes current in Israel."[29] Christology developed later.

Farrer clearly upholds the fullness and significance of Jesus's human life. Jesus grew from childhood to adulthood and experienced "spiritual enlargement." He grew in his capacity for the outpouring of the Holy Spirit: "The infant Jesus lacked nothing of what his little heart was able to receive; the growing boy was capable of more, the grown man of more again."[30] The human decisions and actions of the grown man Jesus were memorable and life changing for those who came to know him. "The spontaneity of his compassion moves us to tears," Farrer states. "The blaze of his indignation shocks us; his speech is an unforced poetry, the coinage of his heart; the sacrifice on which he spent his blood was a decision personally made in agonies of sweat." Through all of Jesus's human expressions and actions, his lasting impression on his friends was that "his whole life was the pure and simple act of God."[31] Jesus incarnates divine life and love.

The incarnation of God in Christ makes God available to humanity for salvation in ways that we can perceive and understand. In the sermon "Messianic Prophecy and Preparation for Christ," Farrer states that "the incarnation brings the saving power and presence of God down into the world at a particular place, where we can have union with him, to our everlasting advantage." In this way, the incarnation fulfils the human aspiration "of finding God in some defined or covenanted person or place, so as to have union with his life, and blessings from his hand."[32] The incarnation accommodates God to humanity so that the divine hope may be known in ordinary life.

Farrer states that in seeing how Jesus "is minded towards mankind, we see our God, and the mind of God towards us. Seeing how He is minded towards His Father, we see the pattern of our obedience."[33] Jesus reveals the loving Father and fully obedient humanity. He taught that we "cannot ask too much of God," so long as our asking is done in obedience to divine providence and not in challenge.[34] Indeed, for Jesus, being "the Son of God is to be perfect in obedience."[35] Jesus incarnates human obedience to God.

Jesus Christ provides the "perfect expression" of "the human pole of the relation between God and man, as redemption restores it under the conditions of our present life."[36] In Christ "there is the true man truly responding to the true God with true humanity." Christ's humanity "is itself human nature perfectly actualized in its true setting, that of absolute rightness of relation towards God." Therefore, what happens in Christ "is what happens, however imperfectly, in believers."[37] Jesus incarnates right relationship with God.

In death (the result of his obedience), Jesus shared fully in the human life experience to its natural end. As "we go to pieces bodily" when we die, so it was for

Jesus, who "went to pieces in that human life he had taken" and "would not be spared anything that belongs to our common lot." Encountering death, Jesus "trusted, as we all must trust, his Father to take the pieces up, and put them together again."[38] In a similar way, Episcopal priest James DeKoven (1831–79) states that there is hope for "gathering up the fragments" of a human life in Christ.[39] Jesus faced the worst of human experience with perfect trust in God and perfect obedience. Trust, for Jesus, "is the rule of faith."[40] The trust in God that Jesus incarnates is the trust that Christians are called to live.

As Jesus shared the human experience of death, he also revealed and opened to us the human experience of resurrection. Indeed, Farrer states in the essay "Eucharist and Church in the New Testament" that "the whole of the divine purpose for the creation was implicit in Christ."[41] Farrer describes Christ's resurrection as a "shattering paradox" that "spliced the new creation into the old, and grafted eternity on time."[42] "Jesus," he writes, "always received what he bestowed and underwent what he redeemed. He who delivers from death died, he who gives resurrection rose from the dead; he who saves in temptation was tempted, he who baptizes was baptized."[43] In Christ's resurrection, "God has given us our only sufficient pledge: what he will do for all in the end and out of this world, he did for Jesus in this world and as it were by anticipation."[44] Jesus lives through death and incarnates resurrection.

The event of Christ's resurrection was "clean beyond the natural order," neither contrary to nor in accordance with the natural order, and it manifested the truth that "God who made us and all things can continue, renew and enrich our being in another sort of life if he chooses; and he chooses."[45] Resurrection life is supernatural, and it is available to us through faith in Christ.

Farrer states that the resurrected Jesus has a human need for others. Jesus is "more of a man, not less of one, by having died and risen," so that the resurrected Jesus needs others "not less, but more" to "continue his divinely human life." He experiences an unlimited "range of fellowship" but is still "only Jesus by what his friendship does in human souls, whether those souls are on earth or in heaven."[46] Being human, like love itself, is relational. This was true for Jesus in his mortal life, and it is true now, in his resurrection. Death, Farrer explains, "cuts us off from company," but resurrection "restores us to fellowship with the living." It is no surprise that Jesus was "no sooner risen from the dead than he was among his disciples," since he was "the first to die of the divine fellowship" and "none of his human friends were in heaven."[47]

Jesus's life of self-emptying sacrifice and death on the cross was at the heart of what it meant for him to be the Christ. He "had rehearsed his death continually; not morbidly, but with joy and self-forgetfulness," and his "passion was no more than the last expression of what he had done all his life."[48] It was Jesus's human vocation and identity. The cross was the ultimate Christian paradox and contradiction—power in helplessness, victory in humiliation, life in death.

The cross, Farrer states, "closed the scene which the manger had opened, the powerlessness of infancy was crowned by the powerlessness of defeat, and the unconscious agony of birth by a conscious agony of dying."[49] Unlike the waffling and ambivalent resolutions that we make (and withdraw), Jesus's death on the cross "was a self-giving final and absolute."[50] Farrer even states that the whole of Christian religion is "summed up in two pictures: God the creator breathing into man's nostrils the breath of life, God the redeemer dying for man on the cross, and breathing out his life into the keeping of his Father." These are "the two poles of our faith, and each of them is God."[51]

But Farrer is quick to emphasize that the cross was not just for Jesus; it is for all who believe in him and follow his way. Christians must undergo crucifixion of the will to follow Christ, so that "our most uncrucified will is reunited with the cross" and "we are forgiven and accepted as living parts of Christ."[52] The divine-human relationship must be fulfilled humanly in each Christian life, and Jesus shows the way for this fulfilment.

Farrer states that there is much more to Christian faith than the development of our human potential for happy living. With respect to "our dear, delightful, unconverted friends," we may affirm that "they are splendid manifestations of the power to live, but that they have not yet learned to die, they have not made even the first step along that more difficult path which Jesus Christ opened up for us." The obstacles of self must be removed for faith to be fulfilled. For the unconverted as for the faithful, Farrer states, it is necessary for them "not merely to undergo death, they have to achieve death, have to make a positive use of death, to throw off their self-bound being so that God may receive a willing material for his own love to remake."[53] Ironically, in terms of human living and dying, the dying must come first for Christian living. Farrer states that "we must die before we can live, abandon what we are and ask to be reborn; and of this process there is no end." Our own dying and our own resurrection in the life and love of God must occur daily.[54]

God desires that "we should grow, live, expand, enrich our minds and our imaginations, become splendid creatures." But God "also desires that we should die, should be crucified on the cross of Christ Jesus, should surrender all we have and are to him." Of course, the encounter with death is inevitable for us. The only question is *when* we will face it, "in this world or the next." God "desires that we should die that death spiritually before we have to die it physically." For us "truly to fear God, to reverence him as his holiness demands," Farrer urges, "is to make a complete sacrifice of ourselves to him. There is no fear of God that stops short of that." The only way this can happen is by our sharing in the cross of Christ, so that "we say to Christ, 'Take me, crucify me on your cross, for I cannot do the crucifying for myself. Make my sacrifice part of your sacrifice, nail me to it and do not let me slip.'"[55] We may share salvation in Christ as we share his cross.

The daily dying to the self and the selfish will is no easy process, and many have difficulty understanding the meaning of the cross of Christ. Our experience of the cross is not just the consequence of living dangerously or of taking risks for possible gains to serve our interests, as in "nothing venture, nothing win." That would be "worldly wisdom," Farrer states. The cross is not the painful consequence of a losing gamble. Instead, "Christ says, 'Come and be hanged'; and that is no sort of worldly wisdom."[56] By the cross we offer our lives, share Christ's sacrifice, and give up everything that thwarts God's love for us.

The good news about human suffering is that it is redemptive, and we need not suffer alone. Our suffering is shared directly by Christ, who "is every sufferer, every child."[57] It is by the "breaking of our heart" that we receive adoption as the children of God.[58] Farrer explains "the gospel of Christ's Passion" is that "God saves us not only out of suffering, but by suffering." The sufferings of Christ redeem the world, "and his sufferings work out their divine effects through the sufferings of Christians."[59] We cannot overcome the evils in our lives by running away from them, but "it is our faith that in standing against them we can vanquish them, through our union with the heroic and all-conquering Passion of Christ."[60] It is the cross of Christ *in our lives* that saves us. For us to experience an "everlasting end," it is necessary to be emptied of ourselves and "filled with God," so that all is "caught up and transformed in that death and resurrection which Christ fulfilled for us."[61] By the cross we may share salvation in Christ.

The Holy Spirit (Pneumatology)

The activity of the Holy Spirit in the world is intimately related to the activity of Christ, as Jesus's own earthly life was filled and fulfilled by the Spirit. Jesus was given by God the Father "an infinite capacity to receive his Father's life; and that capacity is always infinitely fulfilled by the inflow of his Father's Spirit." As Jesus grew, his human capacity and receiving of the Father's life by the Spirit also grew.[62] Even if Jesus "promises the Paraclete as a second self, as an overflow of Christ" in the Last Supper discourses in the Gospel of John, it was Jesus himself who "lived first in the very overflow of God," living in the Spirit.[63] Jesus needed the inspiration of the Holy Spirit, he was filled with the Holy Spirit, and he spread the inspiration of the Holy Spirit to his disciples "in proportion as they came, by adoption, to partake in his Sonship." Jesus shared the life he was living with his disciples, a life fully inspired by the Holy Spirit, as his sonship was "a continual dependence on his Father's Spirit."[64]

The Holy Spirit is to be understood in Trinitarian terms. The "two acts of God the Father" are "to beget and to bestow," and neither act is "conceivable without the other." God the Father begets the Son and bestows the Holy Spirit on the Son. In this regard, "what is begotten is God, and what is bestowed is equally God." Farrer clearly upholds the full divinity of Son and Holy Spirit, stating that "here is one Godhead which can be what it essentially is, a society of Love, only through distribution in three Persons." Specifically, it is the Spirit who "enjoys perfection in being perfectly bestowed on a perfect recipient by a perfect giver."[65]

It is likewise the Spirit who inspires humanity. Farrer states that "if we answer divine love it is by divine inspiration." But Christ is the only perfect recipient of divine inspiration, and our humanity is the limiting factor for the Spirit's activity in us. Farrer notes that "the Holy Ghost is measured in us by the narrowness of our vessel, to the Eternal Son he gives himself without measure. The Son does not measure the Spirit by limiting him, he perfectly expresses him by perfectly receiving him."[66]

It is the Holy Spirit who makes possible our understanding of Christ, as it was the Holy Spirit who inspired understanding in Jesus's "immediate companions." Jesus lived the human life of faith by receiving the Holy Spirit. Similarly, for us and our understanding of Jesus, "God is in us by the Holy Ghost, and therefore we can know incarnate God" in both our historical study of Jesus and in prayer.[67] We may know Christ and live the Christian life of faith by the Spirit.

It is not necessary to seek fantastic experiences to discern the Spirit. As Farrer notes, the "most part of [the Spirit's] action is without any awareness in those he inspires." We cannot "feel" the Spirit, "even when he signifies his action to us by the force and direction he gives to our aspiration." The best way to recognize the presence and activity of the Spirit is not by special feelings or emotions but by the effects discerned in human lives. The Spirit's presence is to transform our lives, not to thrill us. As with the saints who may have been "engrossed with the people who drew forth their charitable concern" and "least aware" of the activity of the Spirit in their lives, Farrer states that "where there is the self-forgetting charity of the saints, there, surely, is the Holy Ghost."[68] The Spirit is revealed in the expression of God's love.

The Spirit centers us beyond ourselves, "in the heart of God."[69] The Spirit is "the imparted love of God," who inspires love.[70] The Spirit empowers our response of love to the divine presence in our lives. As "love has come down to us, the heart of heaven is here." Farrer declares that "it is with the impulse of the Holy Ghost, and by the leading of the Eternal Son, that we give the Father of our lives our hearts."[71] Living the Christian life is made possible by the Spirit.

Human participation in the divine activity of the Holy Spirit is a matter of life or death. "'Holy Ghost' means 'divine life bestowed,'"[72] Farrer states. In this light, "the difference between a real God and an edifying fiction" is plain, because "no edifying fiction raises the dead." The question is one of "death, and the Holy Ghost," because in death "no moving power in our own hearts or wills is going to raise us from our dust." We cannot save ourselves. Our hope and salvation are in the divine activity of the Spirit, and "we must be born again."[73]

The Church (Ecclesiology)

The church's "first mission," according to Farrer, "is to re-create the right relation with God, or rather to be the instrument of God for such a work."[74] The church is empowered for life and ministry by the Holy Spirit, whose divine activity is loving and "corporative."[75] That is, the Spirit draws together and sends out the church into the world, incorporating many members into the one body of Christ. Farrer states that when he leads the church's prayers of intercession, he goes through the motions and speaks the words, but God gives the Spirit and the church prays in the Spirit. The church's prayers include many good requests—"for sun and rain, for plenty and for peace, for everything it is wholesome and natural we should desire"—including the prayer that "the undertakings our wishes prompt, may be prayed into harmony with almighty love, through the Spirit that lurks in us."[76] The Spirit's activity in the church's prayers is not for the sake of giving us whatever we desire. The Spirit guides us into sharing the truth and life of God's love.

Farrer is clear that the Spirit is active in the church, but not confined by the church. It would be "a subject of the greatest difficulty" to define exactly the extent that "the Spirit moulds his action upon the form of the Church." The Spirit does this "in some manner," but "no Christians suppose him to be bound by the physical limits and lineaments of the Church." Relative to the Spirit's activity in and beyond the church, Farrer adds that "the sacraments are covenanted mercies; of uncovenanted mercies the number is infinite, and the scope unknown."[77]

Farrer strongly emphasizes the corporate nature of the church as the connected fellowship of believers who share life in Christ. Of course, as individuals we "have to go on our own feet," but—and here Farrer uses a mountain climbing analogy— "we climb together as alpinists do, bound in one chain by the mutual working of common faith." We are not alone in our faith. Farrer's analogy provides a warning, however, for "if any of us fails to cooperate, he does not merely spoil his own life, he betrays the common endeavor and weakens all other believers."[78] The Christian faith is diminished when anyone withdraws from others in the church. We are not alone in our faith, and we are not called to a lonely spiritual quest.

Farrer states that "we are all responsible for one another's happiness; and we are bound, as Christians, to pay regard to the providences by which God puts us in one another's way and makes us one another's concern."[79] The Christian faith is not to be lived in isolation. We are not to "creep into a quiet corner" to make our individual peace with God, we are to engage the Christian life tangibly in and through the church, "for the Christ who turns your face to his own is still in the world and you must meet him there." Until we surrender to Christ's human body, the church, we are "not reconciled to his divine person."[80]

The members of the church are members of Christ and "dying members as soon as they become detached from the body and from the head" because "we have no life in ourselves."[81] We share living faith in communion with other Christians because our communion is with Christ, whose "dying and rising faith" overflows and runs "in the veins" of all Christians.[82] The church provides us fellowship with Christ, and with others in Christ, and fellowship is precisely what we need. It is a matter of life or death. "Life has to be shared," Farrer warns, "or it doesn't even live." Even God's own Trinitarian life is relational; and, similarly, we are to share "a fellowship with human friends, which is to be at the same time a fellowship with the persons of the Godhead."[83] We may find and be found by God through others.

The Christian fellowship is a unity of love that brings with it abundant love and abundant responsibilities. By making us "living parts of his worshipping body," Christ takes us up into his perfect worship of God the Father.[84] Because Christ is in us and we are in Christ, God's delight for each of us is "immeasurable."[85] But just as we have been taken as friends into Christ's heart, "it is the living out of our unity in Christ, that we should care for one another with the heart of Christ, and by our prayers throw ourselves into the deepest concerns of our friends."[86] Living friendship with Christ means living friendship with others, which is the life of the church.

It would be wrong to imagine that we are "separate units" who communicate by "signalling to one another across physical spaces by physical signs." We are not reduced by faith to islands of individuality. Instead, "our prayers invade and enliven one another," and we share with one another as Christ shares with us "to be the heart in that community of spiritual creatures which serves the Father Almighty."[87] Christ's presence is the heart of the church as living spiritual community.

Farrer likewise emphasizes Christ's active presence as central to the reality and power of the sacraments. The "special mercy of Christ to us in the Sacraments" is that "he just puts himself there," not making his presence in the sacraments "depend on anything special in us who receive," or anything special in the elements such as the bread and wine, or anything special in the priest. Christ's sacramental presence is a gift. God "does not wait for our dignity or our perfection." The sacraments "grow on the great branching tree of the Apostles' ministry," which is "the tree planted by Christ."[88] Christ is the source and power of the sacraments, as he is the source and power of the church, which makes the sacraments available.

Christ "causes in us what he himself undergoes," so that "in the matter of baptism, he is the regeneration by water and Spirit."[89] It is only in Christ that we receive and share the benefits of baptism. Farrer states that "we cannot be baptized without being baptized into [Christ's] baptism: and the unity we have with him both in receiving baptism and afterwards in standing by it, brings down on us the very blessing and the very Spirit he received."[90] The faithful are to know the life of Christ through the sacraments of the church. We should, Farrer declares, "bathe in the waters of her font as in the stream that flowed from Christ's side, take the bread as his body, hear the absolution as from his lips."[91]

Speaking to the congregation as celebrant at the Eucharist, Farrer states that "as I move about the altar, as I break and give the bread, I am still dancing myself and you into sympathy with the heart behind the world."[92] Our sacramental participation in the life of the church is all about our life in Christ and Christ's life in us, so that we may find ourselves increasingly "danced into sympathy with the heart behind the world." With respect to the Eucharist, Farrer states that as Christians feed on Christ and have union with Christ in the sacrament, "we have union with all his people, all his mystical body."[93]

The "content of the New Testament Gospel is expressed, summed and mediated by the Eucharist in the Church."[94] The Christian communion "is held together most of the time by prayer, ordinary companionship, and sheer faith in a bond invisible, which Christ sustains, not we." Our communion with Christ is ongoing. It is our environment, surrounding us constantly, like the air or the "water in which we swim." The Christian communion is "visibly manifested and physically united" at the Sunday Eucharist.[95] The Eucharist is the visible communion of the church. Christ, Farrer explains, is the power and the meaning of the Eucharist, which "just is our religion, sacramentally enacted." Indeed, the whole of Christianity "is summed up in Christ," with "no aspect of it" left out, and the Eucharist "presents Christ, his birth, death, resurrection, and his present existence: his manhood and his godhead, his being in himself, and the service of his Father."[96] The Eucharist makes Christ visible.

At its most basic level, the bread of the Eucharist shared by the community gathered provides "the immemorial bond of common food," so that "those who build their bodies from one loaf are one body; just as those who draw their being from common parents are one blood."[97] Those who share the blessed bread "have their common existence from a common stock."[98] Of course, when Christians share the bread of the Eucharist, "we do not merely stock our bodies from the same stuff as Jesus used for stocking his." Sharing the Eucharist is sharing the life of Christ. The Eucharistic bread is Jesus's body. Christians feed on him and are united by his body. "Lift up your hearts," Farrer prays, "by this sacrament you are parts of Christ, and Christ is the heart of heaven."[99]

Farrer's understanding of sacramental theology translates directly into application for Christian living. Concerning the Eucharist, Farrer states that "if Christ offers us up with his own death in this sacrament, it is that we may die a voluntary and daily death, and merit a daily resurrection."[100] Even when we leave the altar, we "ask for our smouldering sacramental faith to be blown into a flame."

Farrer states that all our prayer and obedience are one with the Eucharist and "participation in Christ's dying love."[101]

In the Eucharist we receive Jesus in our mouths and hearts, so that "we may go and be Jesus in our place and calling, and in relation to all those with whom we have to do."[102] Bodily, we are to share the eucharistic sacrifice. Christ "blessed no bread that he did not break," and *we* are included in the body and bread that was broken, so that "in sacrificing himself [Christ] sacrificed us."[103] The Eucharist is a lived sacrifice for those who share it.

Farrer states that by the power of the Spirit, "divine generosity makes us bodily members of Christ's body" and "bodily parts of Christ's acceptable offering," so that "through the power of the same Spirit, we may make our self-sacrifice effective, or rather, allow Christ to work out his sacrifice in us and work us into his sacrifice."[104] The dying and rising that is at the heart of the Eucharist is to be lived daily by Christians. Concerning the "social" Eucharist, Farrer states that "to live in Christ is to die to flesh and self: but it is also to live for the members in the body."[105] In this sense, there is no private communion to be experienced in isolation from others.

A particular ethical application Farrer identified for the church concerns openness—to doubts, questions, differences of opinion and perspective. He warns that "the spirit of faction, and of that self-hatred which is the twin of self-righteousness, can so bedevil religion as to make it a form of positive evil, and a blinding of the heart." In this light, religious believers are often seen by the world as "grinders of axes" who do not judge with "unbiased appreciation" due to "fear of disturbing their prejudices or cherished beliefs."[106]

Farrer strongly criticizes "the cowardice, the unwholesomeness, the stupidity and the implicit lack of faith" of some at Oxford University who were "going about here and advising their friends never to think or study along any line which raises religious doubt." The "worst" advice for an inquiring mind, Farrer states, "is to try not to think." He offered advice that was "positive, not negative," urging his hearers not to run away from "disquieting considerations" but to "feed your soul on God" and believe that "God is able to persuade you of his own truth by the revelation he has made."[107] The church may even learn something true and valuable from surprising sources. For example, it would be well, Farrer states, for the church to listen even to "our own heretics" and seek to understand what drove them into heresy, instead of being most concerned to condemn and suppress them.[108] The church "need be afraid of no questionings," Farrer states, "as long as you allow a fair field and no favor" and do not weight the scale against faith.[109]

In this regard, Farrer is close to the Episcopal theologian William Porcher Du-Bose, who states that "the truth, which won consent in the past after the freest discussion, has nothing to fear from the unrestrained criticism of the present. It can safely be trusted to defend itself, if the field is left open."[110] The church has nothing to fear from the truth and may affirm the truth wherever it is found. DuBose states that "truth is only made known and indeed only knows itself in conflict with error." The "collective mind of the church," he explains, "sooner or later excludes what is spiritually false and includes what is spiritually true."[111] DuBose "strove earnestly to reassure the authorities of the Church who were trembling for the safety of the Ark of God."[112] Farrer likewise reassured those who "trembled" for the safety of the church in his own day at Oxford, and he called the church to face the challenges and questions that arise in each era.

Austin Farrer as a youth. Reproduced by the kind permission of the Warden and Fellows of Keble College, Oxford University

Farrer as an under-graduate at Balliol College, Oxford, between 1923 and 1926. Used with the kind permission of the Trustees of the K. D. Farrer Trust and with permission of Caroline Farrer and Nick Newton

Farrer in 1928. Used with the kind permission of the Trustees of the K. D. Farrer Trust and with permission of Caroline Farrer and Nick Newton

Austin and Katharine Farrer at their wedding on April 15, 1937. The Bodleian Library, University of Oxford, Farrer Papers (Box 11). Used with the kind permission of the Trustees of the K. D. Farrer Trust and with permission of Caroline Farrer and Nick Newton

Katharine at St. Anne's College, Oxford, in 1932 or 1933. Used with the kind permission of the Trustees of the K. D. Farrer Trust and with permission of Caroline Farrer and Nick Newton

Katharine Farrer in 1951. Used with the kind permission of the Trustees of the K. D. Farrer Trust and with permission of Caroline Farrer and Nick Newton

Farrer with Katharine and Caroline at the wedding of Arthur and Pamela Newton in 1948. Katharine was Arthur Newton's elder sister. Used with the kind permission of the Trustees of the K. D. Farrer Trust and with permission of Caroline Farrer and Nick Newton

Austin Farrer (right) with Arthur Vogel at Nashotah House, an Episcopal seminary in Nashotah, Wisconsin, in front of the "Preaching Cross." Vogel was professor of systematic theology at Nashotah House and later bishop of West Missouri. Used with the kind permission of the Trustees of the K. D. Farrer Trust and with permission of Caroline Farrer and Nick Newton

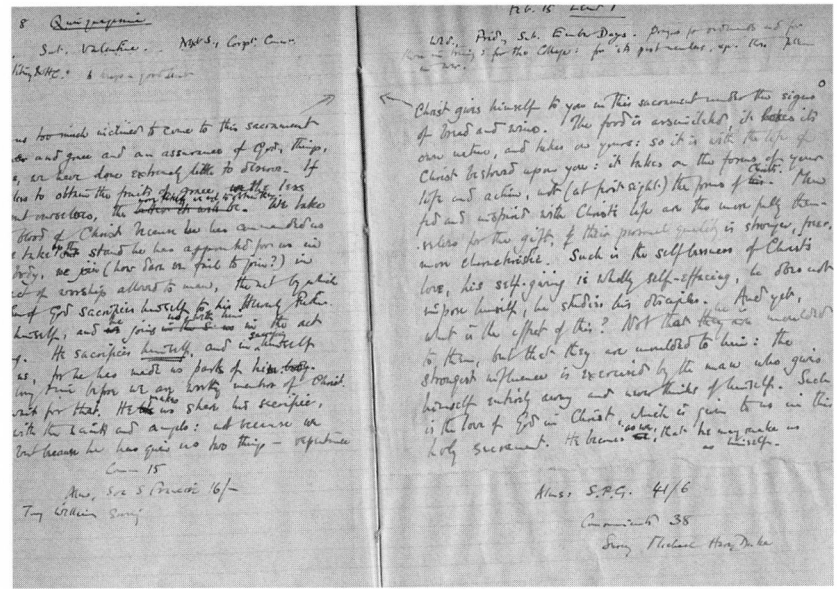

Holograph of a homily by Austin Farrer for the First Sunday in Lent, February 15, 1959. Used with the kind permission of the Trustees of the K. D. Farrer Trust, and with permission of Caroline Farrer and Nick Newton. Manuscript on deposit in the Modern Papers and John Johnson Reading Room, Department of Special Collections and Western Manuscripts, New Bodleian Library, University of Oxford, on behalf of the K. D. Farrer Trust

Trinity College Chapel, Oxford. Photograph by the author

Keble College Chapel, Oxford. Photograph by the author

Detail of exterior design of Keble College. Photograph by author

3

The Ultimate Hope

The Lord's Prayer speaks of the ultimate Christian hope: the coming of God's kingdom on earth as in heaven. The liturgical season of Advent celebrates the church's expectancy, and the catechism of the Episcopal Book of Common Prayer concludes with a section concerning this hope, which is "to await the coming of Christ in glory, and the completion of God's purpose for the world."[1] Farrer states that "God has put his infinity in our mind, and if we cannot stretch out for him beyond the little beginnings here allowed us, we must let go of God and lose him wholly."[2] Indeed, Farrer declares, "Christ in glory is the heart of heaven, and it is difficult to see how those Christians who leave the life to come an open question can be Christians at all."[3] It is only God who "can give us a future," and belief in resurrection is the "acid test" of belief in God. A "God who raises the dead is a real power; he is not just a fanciful name for the order of nature, whether physical or moral," Farrer states.[4] The Christian hope is at the heart of Christian faith.

Unfortunately the doctrine of the last things, or eschatology, has been neglected as an area of theology as well as in the life of the church. This neglect can cause the church to be backward looking. Appreciating destination in terms of hope for the future has everything to say about Christian living today. For Farrer, hope "involves some real confidence in a good to come, or a good which cannot be defeated," although hope "does not pin her faith to the success of any single expectation."[5]

With respect to heaven as our future in God, Farrer warns that it is "a state of being, to us unknown"[6] and that "our pictures of heaven are all of them false." Farrer certainly claims no vision or previously unrevealed knowledge of heavenly reality, but he offers some specific descriptions of what heavenly life will be. If the eschatological future seems daunting and unknown, he assures the church that it is shaped by Christ and known in Christ. Farrer states that "the entry of God into the world in Christ, and our being by the Spirit enabled to know Him there, is the actual revelation of our end; and it is from our end that we know our true 'nature.'"[7] As the true nature of an acorn may be seen in a fully grown oak, its intended end, Christ likewise reveals the true nature, end, and fulfilment of humanity.[8]

Farrer states that in the presence of Jesus in the world, we see "prefigured" the cross and the resurrection, and the mission of the church to all people. They are all of one piece. "The act of charity which healed the sick was identical in essence with the act of charity which consented to die for sinners," Farrer notes. Therefore we may understand that "Christ's healing virtue was a manifestation of the power which emptied the Easter sepulchre."[9] That is Christ's "Way," and it is meant to be shared. The destiny of humanity is also to suffer and die, and "only so" to enter into glory.[10]

Participation in Jesus's way is freely available, but it includes suffering and costs everything. After Peter confessed Jesus to be the Christ, Jesus silenced him and the other disciples. This silencing, "until the Son of Man shall have arisen from the dead," is not just a "political precaution" or an instruction based on the fear "they will blurt out the truth unseasonably," Farrer states. Rather, the disciples were silenced because "all testimony to Christ has a tinge of the satanic, if the witness is not prepared to witness with his life." In this regard, Peter thought "he could witness with his life on the road to Gethsemane, but in the High Priest's courtyard he found that he could not."[11] Here, as in other writings, Farrer is uncompromising in his presentation of the demands and sacrifices of the Christian life.

The Foretaste of Heaven, Already but Not Yet Fully Known

Heaven is not just about fulfilling our wishes, giving us shirts "whiter than the latest detergent can wash them" or light without electricity. But heaven can be known now, at least in part, at least in foretaste. Farrer states:

> It is not silly to say, "Every now and then, perhaps, I manage to be at the disposal of God's will. How marvellous to be in heaven! I shall live in it all the time." Nor is it silly to say, "From time to time I think I catch a glimpse of what God is doing. How marvellous to be in heaven! I shall see his purposes in everything, as clearly as I read my friends' feelings on their faces." Nor is it silly to say, "Every now and then I see a bit of what God has put into the people round me. How marvellous to be in heaven! I shall see it all."[12]

Concerning the marvels of being in heaven, Farrer concludes that (1) "they are joys of which we have a foretaste in this life," (2) "they are joys which arise from a more perfect relation with realities—with God and with the children of God," and (3) "they are joys which might be actualized (for anything we know) under a variety of conditions, or states of being." That is, "our faith in heaven is a confidence in the pattern of perfect relations; as for the state of being, we can leave it to God."[13] We can be sure that our heavenly life is the perfection and completion of our relational life with God and with others in God, in the "pattern of perfect relations," even if the specifics of that heavenly state of being are unknown to us now and must be left to God.

The life and love of God that is known today—through word and sacrament, friends and family, ministry and service—is the real item. No one must wait to "go" to heaven or anywhere else to receive God's love. Indeed, Farrer states, "heaven is God."[14] We already know it, but not yet in its fullness. That comes later, in the future. For now, we see "through a glass, darkly."[15] Heaven is available now in an already-but-not-yet kind of way. Farrer states that "we have met God, and we have God to meet."[16] God's glories are hidden, but we may know them by faith and God's word. We may know God's glories now in a way that is effective, if incomplete. As Farrer prays, "Even now we do not receive your promises as sounds in our ears lacking present effect. For the word and the Spirit by which you assure us of felicity to come are the beginning and foretaste of what they foretell."[17] The foretaste of God's glory is a real taste, and we may anticipate its future completion in our lives.

The Christian faith is oriented toward fulfilment in the future, beyond both the limitations and possibilities of the present. Christian faith is more than "a this-worldly religion" with the chance of "a bonus hereafter." Offering an analogy—that of standing outside a door and seeking entrance—Farrer states that for now "it is a marvellous thing to have been admitted so far, to have a crack of the door open, and half a foot on the sill; but it is always in the future, that we shall make something of the beginning which has been so mercifully allowed to us."[18] It is wonderful to behold the opening door of divine love, but we may anticipate love's fulfilment as we enter fully over the threshold we have seen.

Heaven and Relationship

In his writings, Farrer suggests many ways to understand heaven, but the focus of "our ideas of heaven are bound to be ideas of a relation to God."[19] Indeed, "Christ in glory is the heart of heaven."[20] Farrer's understanding of heaven does not focus on God in isolation. As with much else in Farrer's work, his understanding of heaven has to do not only with God but also with how the heavenly relationship with God carries over into our relationships with others. For those who know the heavenly glory of God, their openness to God comes with "a natural response on their own part," so that "they cannot feel the heart of God, and not themselves share his love for a thousand other happy creatures." Similarly, "they cannot know the will of God, without performing it, in all the splendid works that he has designed for them to do."[21] Heaven is to be known and shared with others in the daily contexts of life.

Farrer describes heaven in terms of relational possibilities we have never known previously. The greatest of blessings will be "a direct, unclouded perception of God himself," including experience of "all the greatness of his mercy."[22] In heaven, God's purposes become "immediately visible," and "we have no distinction to make between the divine thought and its effect in us."[23] Farrer also states that in heaven "the obstacles to one man's knowing a multitude of individuals are done away."[24] Heaven will mean a closeness of community with others that we have never before experienced. "Even in heaven," Farrer states, "we shall keep a fellow-feeling for our own kind," and we "shall not be able, even, to delight in God himself, without calling in our friends to share our delight, while we also delight in their delighting." In heaven we will surpass the limitations and falseness of human relationships as we have known them. In heaven "we shall read one another's hearts, and have no need of those natural veils and cultivated reserves, which in this earthly life mask shame, disguise ill-nature, or cover emptiness."[25] The artificial barriers that separate us from one another will be removed. Similarly, the "very essence" of the church's heavenly fulfilment "is the co-existence of fellowship and universality. The limitations of time and space are annihilated, in order that all the blessed may be found in the immediate presence of God and of one another."[26] Heaven will be the fulfilment of relationship with God and others who share the divine life without impediment or barrier.

The human future in God is beyond us, and it is relational. The human "calling and destiny" is "primarily to be divinized; to be adopted into union with God, and made one with his heart."[27] Heaven is not to be understood as "a place for one glorified man, and for no more."[28] It is not a place of isolation, not even a divine isolation. "Heaven consists essentially of its citizens," Farrer states, "not of jasper bulwarks, or pavements of transparent gold." Heaven is relational, just as the end of humanity is "social."[29]

Farrer states that "a heaven of souls without Christ would not be heaven," and likewise, rhetorically, he asks, "Could we not say the same about a heaven of Christ without souls?" As "Christ's incarnation would have been nothing, but for his relation to his family, his disciples, and his nation; his continued incarnation after he rose would have been nothing but for his continuing relation with those he left on earth." Christ's resurrection was not an event in isolation from those who shared his love. His human relationships continued in his resurrection, revealing a love stronger than death. Indeed Christ's mystical body was built up as others joined him in glory, forming "the nucleus of heaven, and the instrument of universal redemption."[30] Farrer states again and again that the heavenly reality (like the human reality) is relational and meant to be shared with others. "Christ is not only God in man," Farrer asserts, "he is God in mankind; God in one man isolated from all others would not even be God in man, for a man in isolation is not a human possibility."[31] And heaven in a divine isolation is not an eschatological possibility.

Apocalypse and Passion

If we wonder about the Last Things, the End Times, heaven, we may discern their nature in Christ—particularly in the passion. Farrer states that the quality of Christ's love "is tasted and the substance apprehended in the earthly history of his passion."[32] The "desolating abomination" of the End Times was visible to Christ's eleven disciples in the garden of Gethsemane,[33] and "when the disciples saw the abomination, they were in the field, and they fled fast enough."[34] Farrer states that "the substance of the Last Things and the substance of the Passion are one and the same."[35] The cross reveals the End. Farrer substantiates his point by drawing out the parallels between Jesus's warning concerning the End Times ("watch, therefore, for you know not when the master of the house cometh, whether late, or in deep night, or at cockcrow, or early, lest coming suddenly he find you sleeping")[36] and the events leading up to the passion:

> When it is *late,* they sit at supper with Jesus and learn that a traitor is in their midst. When it is (evidently) *deep night,* they cannot watch, he comes to them again and again in Gethsemane and finds them sleeping. The armed men appear, the eleven run for their lives. When *the cocks are crowing* Jesus, arraigned before the High Priest, confesses, and Peter in the court below denies. When it is *early,* Christ faces Pilate alone.[37]

In these ways, Farrer concludes, the pattern and the substance of the apocalypse take firm hold on the story of the passion.[38] The apocalypse and the passion indicate the same truth.

The Dimensionality of Heaven

It would be "nonsense" to understand heaven as "a region or even a condition in which the blessed dead find themselves." We do not "enter the presence of God by exchanging life for death as you might enter the presence of a monarch by leaving the anteroom for the throne-room; or as though this world were a shuttered house, and to get out of it were to be in an open air where God is."[39] Instead, Farrer states, heaven is "a created sphere where God bestows his presence by his action, especially his action through heart and mind."[40] This seems to be a shocking speculation, but Farrer explains his understanding of the dimensionality of heaven in light of a pair of traps that lead to misunderstanding the nature of heaven.

On the one hand, Farrer states, if heaven is understood to be nonspatial, "the heavenly life must be a featureless sea of feeling, a shapeless ecstasy; or anyhow, nothing you could fairly call the resurrection-state of man." But on the other hand, "if heaven has any form of spatial dimension, then it falls somewhere in the field of space; a telescope might record it, an astronaut might reach it. And so heaven is pulled back into the perishable universe." Farrer engages this dilemma in a surprising way, drawing on Albert Einstein to describe space as "a web of interactions between material energies which form a system by thus interacting." Therefore, Farrer states, "unless the beings or energies of which heaven is composed are of a sort to interact physically with the energies of our physical world, heaven can be as dimensional as it likes, without ever getting pulled into our spatial field, or having any possible contact with us of any physical kind."[41] Heaven could be dimensional, but in a different dimension from creation as we know it. There would then be no question of finding heaven in outer space, or anywhere else, as an explorer might find an uncharted island in the Pacific Ocean.

Farrer understands heaven to be substantial and dimensional, not an abstraction or a "featureless" goo, yet heaven is most distinguished by the directness and clarity of God's presence. Heaven, he explains, is a "sphere of created being" where God bestows his presence in at least three ways: "by a more visible providence, making the whole order of things the evident expression of an infinite goodness; by a more abundant grace, making the minds of his people transparent to his thought and their hearts to his love; by an incarnate presence with them in the glorified man, Jesus Christ."[42] Heaven is heaven because of the divine presence bestowed by God's actions in particular ways. Heaven is the fulfilment of God's presence.

The Trinity and the Christian Hope

In Christ it is possible to share God's own relational life, which is the Trinity. It is God's fellowship, God's society, God's own life made available in Christ. "Whatever our future hopes," Farrer states, "our present concern is to live ourselves into the living Christ."[43] The Trinity, he explains, "is the substance of personal being and the pattern of personal relation; and it is this substance, this pattern, which God is pleased to reproduce, to represent and to extend in his creation." Christ is "Son-by-Nature" in the Trinity, and "the Son-By-Nature makes us sons-by-adoption through taking our condition and associating us with himself." Christ "lifts us into fellowship with God" and "shares with us the Society which is the divine beatitude."[44] By sharing Christ's life, we engage the divine life of the Trinity.

The Trinity is "that blessed family into which we are adopted," in which "we are made one body with the Son of God, and in him converse with the Eternal Father, through the indwelling of the Holy Ghost."[45] Farrer understands our life,

our future, our hope, and our heaven in relational, triune terms. The Trinity "is
a pattern of life into which we ourselves, by an unspeakable mercy, are taken up."[46]
Therefore, Farrer concludes, "the Trinity is revealed to Christians because they are
taken into the Trinity, because the threefold love of God wraps them round, because it is in the Trinity they have their Christian being."[47]

It is the church, and especially the sacramental life of the church, that extends
Christ's life and the heavenly hope in the present. The "sacramental fellowship is
an anticipation of the Kingdom of God." Farrer states that the "End—the *eschaton*
of eschatological hope—was the restored and glorified Israel of God, a community
gathered round its King and Christ," and that "now the Church of God is the
anticipation of this community, in the Spirit; and is perpetually new-created as
such by communion with her Head in the Eucharist."[48] We may know the Christian hope through the life and sacraments of the church. The Christian hope is
identified with the church and visible in the church.

For Farrer, the "eucharistic sacrifice, always offered and always accepted, con-
veys to us the present being of Christ; not a history of two thousand years ago, but
the act by which he now exists."[49] Christ is understood to be truly present in the
eucharistic moment, a "point of intersection of the timeless / With time," as the
poet T. S. Eliot writes in another context.[50] Edward Yarnold also considers the
making-present of Christ in the Eucharist. He states that Jesus "told his apostles
to 'commemorate' him," and that "in the Bible to recall an event means to bring
it to mind so that it becomes effective." Jesus's "memory was to be made opera-
tive" by the imitation of his actions at the Last Supper. This could mean, Yarnold
explains, that the memory of Jesus was to be an inspiration for the apostles and
others who celebrated the Eucharist, or "that each celebration of the Eucharist was
to make available to the worshippers the fruits of our Lord's Passion."[51] The Christian hope is made present and available at the Eucharist.

With respect to the eucharistic sacrifice, Farrer states that the quality of Christ's
love "is tasted and the substance apprehended in the earthly history of his passion," so that "by bringing down our thoughts to earth, the sacrament sets them
in the heart of heaven."[52] We engage the heavenly hope of Christian faith through
the sacrament of the Eucharist, the extraordinary in the ordinary. In Christianity
a "strangely two-sided symbolism of primitive eucharistic thought" exists. Relative
to the "cornfield parable" and "the mysterious banquets succeeding it," Farrer
explains that "we are what we eat; we eat the bread of God, the body of Jesus, but
at the same time we are a bread of God sown by his word in the field of the world,
gathered into his church and kneaded into one body."[53] In the Eucharist, in Christ,
Christians both receive and live the Christian hope.

Farrer also perceives a parallel between the cornfield parable and the miraculous "multiplication of the loaves," which were "no mere parabolic 'bread' as in the

corn parable." Regarding the numerical proportion of the parable, in which "one seed yields thirty, sixty, or a hundred," and the multiplication of bread, in which "five cakes satisfy not five but five thousand men," he states that "both proportions express the fertility of divine grace in the building up of the Church" and concludes that "the two symbols of the spiritual harvest and of the heavenly bread lay very close to one another in the primitive Christian mind, however hard we may find it to work out a logical relation between them."[54] The Eucharist is foreshadowed by "the miraculous feast which Christ offers to the people," and "the means by which the miracle is performed are simply the eucharistic acts, blessing, breaking, distribution."[55] As stated in the Book of Common Prayer, the Eucharist provides "the foretaste of the heavenly banquet which is our nourishment in eternal life."[56] And so we may see the present eucharistic moment as an "intersection time," anticipated by Christ's own miraculous banquets during his earthly ministry and anticipating the fullness of the heavenly banquet and the eschatological hope of Christian faith.

In terms of baptism, Farrer perceives a relationship between the "legion of demonic swine" who are lost in the waters, the story of the storm "through which divine intervention has brought the disciples safely," and "the waters of the Red Sea, through which Israel was wonderfully brought, and in which the Egyptians drowned." But now "the new exodus delivers not from political, but from spiritual oppression; the enemy is Satan not Pharaoh. And the waters which have to be passed are not the waters of the Red Sea but the waters of the Passion." Even when Christ's disciples panic, he "brings the ark of the Church through," and "in the Passion the whole power of Satan is destroyed." Farrer states that "the waters of the Passion are the waters of baptism, where men are initiated into Christ's death. By that initiation they put the sea of eternal death behind them, and leave their demonic enemies drowning in the font."[57] It is death, not Egyptian soldiers or bad weather, that is overcome by baptism. Healing, too, "corresponds to baptism throughout the Gospel," Farrer notes.[58] Like Cyril of Jerusalem (c. 313–c. 386), who wrote that "Pharaoh was submerged in the sea, and the devil disappears in the waters of salvation," Farrer uses the Exodus story as a type for baptism.[59] In the life of the church, in the sacrament of baptism, it is possible to share the heavenly hope that is rooted in the passion of Christ.

An Earthly and Heavenly Hope

The heavenly reality is beyond but not unrelated to the present world. Farrer states that "the loveliness we have known always increases our desire for the delight to which it points and leads us on."[60] The beauty and goodness that are visible in the world can point us to the fulfillment in God of all beauty and goodness. "Creation, like everything else," Farrer states, "will be perfectly manifest for the first time in heaven."[61] The love that is known and shared in this world points beyond itself to the fulfilment and completion of love in God.

The human "end" is "endless Godhead endlessly possessed."[62] God "wants to make us like himself."[63] Heaven will be "a life in which the very countenance of God is constantly and visibly portrayed in the changing colours of his creatures' lives."[64] The "end of man," as Farrer calls it, our end in God, "flows back in glory on our mortal days, and gives a hope and meaning to whatever Christians do for love of God or love of one another." Human lives and love have an ultimate significance, and "we are all heirs of everlastingness," so that "whatever we do or are furnishes material to the hands which out of perishing stuff create eternal joy."[65] The extraordinary Christian hope may be known in the ordinary circumstances of our lives.

In his last sermon, "The Ultimate Hope," Farrer perceives "two levels of hope" for Christians: "on the short view, hope within the world, that something can be made of it," and on the long view, "hope that what we do in this world is not all going to leak out of the pipe of history into the sands of oblivion." He sharply rejects an either/or way of thinking that would value either the world's future or heavenly bliss but not both at the same time. "Nonsense," Farrer states. "Heaven alone gives final meaning to any earthly hopes; and to take it the other way round, we have no way to grasp at heavenly hope, than by pursuing hopeful tasks here below."[66] We may engage the eschatological reality through present reality.

The heavenly end and future hope give meaning to all that is done and encountered in the present, and the only way to approach and realize the future hope of salvation in Christ is through daily life. In this regard, Farrer agrees with DuBose, who states that we are to be saved through, not from, the experiences of human life in the world: "Life or salvation is not away from the natural to the spiritual, but through and by the natural into the spiritual."[67] The seeds of God's future are in the present, and only through the present is it possible to discover the completion of God's love and the fulfilment of hope.

4

The Problem of Evil

Farrer does not shy away from the difficult questions of life and theology, and perhaps one of the most challenging is the problem of evil. Christians affirm the reality and omnipotence of God in the face of all the bad things that happen in the world, yet the question remains: how can a loving and omnipotent God allow such suffering? Farrer offers a variety of perspectives in his theodices, in which he identifies and praises God's presence in a suffering world and suggests Christian responses in the face of evil.

Evil as Distorted Good

First of all, it should be clear that evils are not sent to us or caused by God. Farrer holds neither God nor the devil responsible for creating evil beings. The "shining excellences that are in mankind themselves create the blackness of a sin which can turn from a realized spiritual beauty to feed on garbage." The "type of sin is not the serpent considered according to its natural kind," Farrer states, "but the rebellious angel who chose to crawl the dust."[1] He understands the patristic position to be that "there are many sorts of things, and each sort, if given its head and allowed to be itself, is good; if warped, spoiled, or inhibited, it is bad."[2]

But none of these "many sorts of things" are evil in themselves. Not everything that happens in the world is "under the hand of almighty providence."[3] God does not punish us with hurricanes or earthquakes. God does not "act like the malicious neighbour in Christ's parable" who scatters tares among the wheat. God does not spread evil in the world. On the contrary, "evils are not *things*. They are unhappy states or misdirected acts of creatures having the capacity for pleasure and for success. Evils do not exist, they happen. They are not created, they are incurred."[4]

There is no need for divine agency to set evils in motion. As Farrer notes, "God does not need to invent temptations for us; the waywardness of our desire, the low standards of our neighbors, the cross-accidents inevitable in a world of creatures freely moving, will provide us enough trials and to spare."[5] In "The Theodicy of Austin Farrer," Simon Oliver observes that Farrer adopted the "Augustinian notion of evil as *privatio boni* and argued that nothing is intrinsically bad. Instead, evil is merely the absence of good and occurs when something fails to be truly itself."[6]

In *Love Almighty and Ills Unlimited*, Farrer offers a humorous illustration to support his assertion that evil is defective good and not its own reality. On "Dr. Sidebottom's Lumbago Powder" we may find the disease of lumbago "represented as a somewhat scraggy little dragon, biting a sufferer in the part affected; while Dr. Sidebottom (if he is the figure with the high collar and the luxuriant mustaches) pitches into the aggressor with an outsized toasting fork."[7]

But this is all allegory. If lumbago were a dragon, Farrer states, it might be "good at being a dragon, but bad for you; while Dr. Sidebottom, if we have to believe him, would, in turn, be bad for it." But "your lumbago is not a dragon— it is only you, or a bit of you, misfunctioning and hurting. To call it bad is to say that it would be good for you neither to hurt nor to misfunction in this way, but to enjoy what you optimistically call your usual health."[8] In other words, lumbago is not a thing in its own right. There would be no lumbago without a healthy body to inflict. Evil is creation's defect, not God's creation.

Farrer also contradicts a dualistic way of thinking that would metaphorically divide the world into a mosaic pavement of black and white marble squares, with each set of squares coming from a different quarry or source. Instead, referencing the patristic tradition and drawing out the image, Farrer states that "the things in the world which we deplore are not to be compared with black squares in a mosaic, but with flawed squares. Some of the marble blocks always had a poor grain and color; others of them have split or crumbled."[9] Therefore, good pieces and bad pieces "are not different sorts; they are perfect and defective examples of the same sort." And disease, in the same way, "is not its own way of being; it is the break-down of health. Evil is essentially the parasite of a good, whose existence it pre-supposes."[10] Badness or evil concerns "the spoiling of a nature, the inhibition of an activity, the frustration of an aim, or the saddening of a[n] existence which we take to be good."[11] Evil is a corrupted good and nothing in itself.

Evil as the Collision or Misfit of Created Systems

Apparent natural evils may be understood as the inevitable collision of different systems in the world and not as intrinsically evil. The universe, Farrer asserts, "isn't *an* organism, or *a* system, or *a* process; it's an unimaginable free-for-all of innu-merable bits of organism, system, process. . . . It's just one damned thing after another."[12] The world, he adds, "is not a system, it is an interaction of systems innumerable"—and those systems inevitably collide. A universe without an inter-ference of systems "would be no physical universe at all." Instead of being "like an animal relieved of pain by the extraction of a thorn," a universe with interference of systems removed "would be like an animal rendered incapable of pain by the removal of its nervous system; that is to say, of its animality."[13] But "when God creates physical creatures," Farrer states, "he lets loose physical forces; and until he dis-creates them again, they will do what they will do."[14] Creation is ongoing and includes collisions. Indeed, creation would in many ways be thwarted or not itself without collisions.

Farrer gives a direct answer to any challenges about the existence of "what men call natural disasters": "God makes the world make itself." In this sense, the world is built up from below. The "multitude of created forces make the world, in the process of making or being themselves. It is this principle of divine action that gives the world such endless vitality, such vital variety in every part." But this vitality and variety comes at a "price." Collisions can be painful, even deadly. Farrer notes in *A Science of God?* that "the agents God employs in the basic levels of the struc-ture will do what they will do, whether human convenience is served by it or not."[15] But the goodness of creation cannot be judged by how well it serves human convenience.

Farrer wonders whether "it would have been possible for God to have made a world without a free-for-all of elemental forces at the bottom of it." Although he does not know the answer to that question, he supposes not, noting that "there is (I take it) only one Mind that does." But he is "convinced that this actual self-making world of ours expresses the will of a Creator," and he thanks God "heartily" for his existence.[16] This world of ongoing creation is a "self-making world" of col-lisions, and it is good, even if we may perceive some of the collisions to be bad.

Whether a system, a creature, a thing, or an agent is acting in a way that is evil or appropriate and constructive would seem to be a matter of perspective. Farrer wonders, rhetorically, whether "when we lament the mutual destructiveness of physical things" we are complaining that "unintelligent creatures are not like vir-tuous men, or indeed, better." Even the best of people cannot extend benevolence "to all the sorts of creatures" around them. Our stomachs, for example, "ruthlessly destroy what they consume, and if we spare animals, we shall still butcher vegeta-bles."[17] We may say that our stomachs are functioning perfectly and just doing their job, but it is a rough job on the thing consumed. Our dietary needs collide with the existence of another thing.

In a similar way, Farrer describes the predations of a ground elder, a "pestilent weed," in a garden. We may say that it is a bad weed. "But when we call it bad," he notes, "we mean it's bad for us, or for the plants we are trying to grow. It's a fine, flourishing thing in itself, and we'd be glad to think of it filling waste land, if it would only keep out of our way."[18] It is a question of perspective whether the ground elder is bad or good. It is bad for the gardener but good for itself (if the ground elder could make such judgments) and, perhaps, even good for a landowner wanting to prevent erosion of uncultivated acreage.

This contrast of perspectives concerning the ground elder allows an important insight into Farrer's understanding of natural evil. He states that "if we say the ground elder is bad for the strawberries, we are not suggesting that the ground elder is capable of good behavior but is, in the present case, behaving badly. We are assuming that the strawberries could be their own excellent selves, but that the ground elder hinders them."[19] What is good for the ground elder may be very bad for the strawberries, but the ground elder is just fulfilling its own nature as a created "action-system," doing what it does or is "apt to do," and it is not in itself evil.[20] The ground elder and the strawberries are systems that collide in creation.

God "does not let natural forces have their heads up to the point only at which their free action would conflict with some fixed principle of higher purpose, for example the welfare and safety of mankind," and then "substitute miracle for nature and stop physical forces from indulging in their characteristic behavior." We should not anticipate such an intervention. For example, Farrer states, an earthquake that "shakes down a city" raises urgent practical problems concerning aid for the survivors and especially the injured, "but no theological problem arises. The will of God expressed in the event is his will for the physical elements in the earth's crust or under it: his will that they should go on being themselves and acting in accordance with their natures."[21] But God did not will the destruction of the city.

The "misfit" or collision of various systems in creation is the natural and inevitable consequence of the physical universe as made by God. Farrer states that "if God was pleased to create a physical universe, he was sure to set going an infinity of forces and a plurality of systems, mostly devoid of intelligence, and acting upon one another in accordance with the limited principle incorporated in each."[22] Collisions, therefore, are inevitable and ongoing in the universe. For example, a plant may die because of inhospitable soil, weeds, or animal pests, but none of these things are evil or bad in themselves, although the consequences for the plant are dire.[23] Of course, circumstances could have been divinely altered to prevent any particular collision or misfit of systems in creation, but this "alteration of the circumstances would have made other accidents." Farrer concludes that "accidentality is inseparable from the character of our universe."[24] The misfit of systems in creation is a matter of natural accident, and the "physical evil" of the collisions of various created systems is inevitable and unavoidable in a created universe.[25]

The Personal Encounter with Evil

Farrer acknowledges the difficulty of facing evil in life, and he considers a variety of perspectives concerning its existence in a world in which God is both creator and actively present. Of all the consolations, he warns, "the promise of an invisible and an eternal good" is "the most glib and the most indecent in the ears of unbelievers."[26] He states that "anyone can spin phrases about a world hidden from sight, where all journeys end, and from which no traveller returns."[27] In the face of another's great personal loss, "however believing we may be, we hesitate to offer open consolations, unless we have an equal right to grief."[28] Farrer recalls that Job's comforters "merited divine rebuke" because they lied, saying that either "our troubles do us good, or they are the just penalty of our faults."[29] Although some evils are "evils in appearance only," it is "the cruelest and most revolting of paradoxes" to "pretend that all evils are merely apparent."[30] Farrer offers no glib assurances in the face of evil.

Farrer himself had to witness the anguish of his friend C. S. Lewis as Lewis faced the terrible death of his beloved wife, Joy, due to cancer.[31] In his contribution for a collection of essays on Lewis, Farrer states that it is not "much good to tell a man labouring to conceive the Providence of God in spite of evils rampant in his Creation, that if after prolonged bachelordom he makes a blissful marriage and loses his wife in a couple of years by an agonizing disease, he will then (should his faith survive) have reason to tell himself that nothing further of the sort is likely to shake it."[32] It is difficult to describe such pain and suffering in optimistic terms.

On the other hand, Farrer imagines a situation in which a child's tragic death causes a change of heart for the parent, though Farrer acknowledges that "it is almost indecent to mention the fact; still more, to dwell upon it with any satisfaction."[33] And yet, the opening of the parent's "narrow heart, being the preparation of a soul for glory and a beginning of heaven on earth, obtains a weight which may fairly tell in the scale of compensations."[34] Good can come out of evil, but there is more at issue than means in service of an end. On the contrary, Farrer states, "good breeds more good than any evil can," and God's "use of evil for good ends does not immediately sterilize it; it continues to breed after its own kind."[35] Evil is still evil, whatever good may ultimately result from it.

God does not create evil for the sake of good. But to say that evil is not from God is not to say that it serves no divine purpose. Human pains can excite divine compassion, as they can "awaken our detestation of their causes" and provoke us to fight them. Shared pain can draw us together and mobilize us for constructive action. "The suffering is felt to be a common evil; and as it moves the sufferer to get rid of the cause in himself, so it moves his kindred to get rid of it for him."[36] The suffering of others can awaken our compassion and move us to help them. Awareness of our own limitation can encourage us to turn to God. Farrer states that "everything which points our insufficiency sharpens our perception of dependence on our all-sufficing God, and leads us home." In this way, "God brings good out of evil and compensates human griefs with divine joys."[37]

Different people respond differently in the face of evil. Some are appalled by "the sight of unassisted misery in others," leading them "to curse or to deny the author of the Universe."[38] For example, after seeing Job's many calamities, his wife urged him to "curse God, and die."[39] But, Farrer observes, those who would deny God after seeing the misery of others "are seldom those who yield to the natural pressure of sorrowful scenes on a compassionate heart, and give themselves to the work of relief." The confrontation with an "overmastering sense of human ills can be taken as the world's invitation to deny her Maker, or it may be taken as God's invitation to succor his world."[40] We can choose our response to the evil we encounter.

Those who "take the practical alternative" and involve themselves in the misery of others will "feel the grain of existence, and the movement of the purposes of God." As they give themselves to love instead of argument, Farrer states, they will discover that as we love more fully, we also feel more deeply "the evils besetting or corrupting the object of our love," and "the more we feel the force of the besetting harms, the more certain we are of the value residing in what they attack; and in resisting them are identified with the action of God, whose mercy is over all flesh."[41] As we resist evils, we can appreciate more fully the goodness of creation (especially the good that we protect) and the activity of the creator. Human virtue is called out and strengthened by resisting and encountering evil. Indeed, resisting evil is a humanizing activity.

In a similar way, William Stringfellow (1928–85) states that during World War II the various activities of underground resistance to the Nazis seemed unlikely to prevail against "the Nazi efficiency and power and violence and vindictiveness," and "those who resisted Nazism did so in an atmosphere in which hope, in its ordinary connotations, had been annihilated." But "in the circumstances of the Nazi tyranny, *resistance became the only human way to live*." This resistance included "abetting escapes, circulating mimeographed news, hiding fugitives, obtaining money or needed documents, engaging in various forms of noncooperation with the authorities."[42] Even if those who resisted could not defeat or repel the Nazis, their acts of resisting evil were humanizing. Confronting evil (which Stringfellow understood as "the power of death") "*is* the definitively humanizing experience," "whatever the apparent outcome."[43]

Relationship and Redemption in the Face of Evil

Christians are not abandoned by God in our suffering or left to tough it out somehow in isolation. Divine compassion means that God "does not desert his creatures in those sufferings which his natural providence allots them, but is with them in providing the deliverance to which the pain excites them."[44] But we may be unable to perceive God's presence and providence in the midst of our suffering. Farrer states that "we ask too much, if we demand that the saving action of God should not only redeem us from sorrow, but should make the redemption to be felt by us in the moment when the sorrow seizes us." We may not feel or recognize God's saving action in the midst of our suffering. In this situation, the one who suffers "needs a faith in the working of particular providence, not a detection of it." The Christian sufferer may not have the sensation of being helped by God. Farrer states that the suffering Christian should simply go on quietly with his or her duties and embrace the "opportunities of well-doing, sustained by the general belief that through these things God will make suffered evils fruitful of good."[45] There may be no quick fix for our sorrows and pains, but we may find God and be found by God through our sorrows and pains.

With or without our understanding, God will work through us and others in the context of our suffering. Farrer states that God's compassion for his suffering creatures is expressed "principally by sustaining and directing the working of their own natures; secondarily by the sympathy of their fellows in those species that are capable of it."[46] God does not prevent all evils, but God is with us and works through us in the face of evil. For all our faith we will "be spared neither pain, sorrow, disappointment, sickness, nor death."[47] Yet we may stand with Christ in his suffering and stand with others in their suffering. In this regard, "suffering is one," and "our endurance assists the endurance of other men, as theirs assists ours," making the sufferer's patience "an unspoken prayer" that will "only gain in force if it finds utterance in intercession."[48] Christians may suffer, regardless of faith, but Christians do not suffer alone.

Instead of a god who sends us pain and misery (which would be a "double torment"), we find relationship with God, who stands with us in the midst of the world's suffering and transforms it. "We begin from a world touched with glories and shot through with agonies, and we call upon the God of glory to deliver us from the wicked fiend," Farrer states.[49] He adds that "acts of life-saving" come straight from the heart of God, but "disaster and destruction are not his in the same way." Bad things in our world may threaten our relationship with God by concealing "the God of love," but they do not "reveal a cruel God."[50]

In the midst of the encounter with evil, it may seem we have been forgotten by God and we may feel very much alone. But in retrospect, we may discern God's "particular providences" and active presence with us in our suffering. "Looking back over a tract of time," Farrer states, "we can see how circumstances have shaped us, even in spite of ourselves, and regret that we have put so many obstacles in the path of a mercy we failed to discern."[51] But we could hardly plan our own way through our suffering, as if "we could have seen the way plain in front of us."

Instead we "could only have found it by letting ourselves be led up it."[52] We may trace the particular providences of the divine that have led us through suffering and along the path of knowing God.

Our suffering is redemptive, and in standing against evils, "we can vanquish them, through our union with the heroic and all-conquering Passion of Christ."[53] It is "the most direct consolation" for the one who suffers to know that his or her suffering "has itself a place in the redemptive action of God." Farrer insists that there is "nothing morbid or masochistic about the doctrine of redemptive suffering."[54] Indeed the gospel of Christ's passion is that "God saves us not only out of suffering but by suffering," that the world is redeemed by Christ's sufferings, and that "his sufferings work out their divine effects through the sufferings of Christians."[55] Christ works for redemption through suffering and stands with Christians who suffer.

Even if the sufferer finds that the "mere supporting of his trouble uses up such energy as he has," the sufferer "is to learn that this mere supporting is a doing, an action of great power, a co-operation with almighty Love." Farrer likens this endurance of the sufferer to the Christian martyrs who "died willingly, to honor and to implement Christ's victory." The martyrs "fought a battle they could not lose, except by their own treason." Although they "were weak in their own strength, they had the grace of God; and nothing could be stronger than omnipotence."[56] Christians who suffer can stand with the martyrs of faith and cooperate in the activity of God's love. We are not to suffer alone.

Evil and the World as It Is

Farrer reminds us that the world is incarnated as it is, created by God as it is, and must be faced by us as it is. In this regard, there is no benefit in wondering "why should Almighty goodness make the world a tangle or, if he made it straight, why should he let it tangle so" or "why God, being perfect, should have given the world the flaws or imperfections that it has." Such questioning merely asks why God did not make the world "otherwise" and "attempts to find a footing on the ground of might-have-beens."[57] These speculations carry us away from reality. We need hardly attempt to "vindicate" God "for making the world as he has made it, rather than otherwise."[58] We have the world as we have it, with all its imperfections.

With respect to Farrer's "philosophical theodicy," Oliver notes G. W. Leibniz's "famous answer" to the question why God created "this physical universe rather than one with less evil": "Given that God could have created any possible world that includes his existence, we must suppose this to be the best of all possible worlds."[59] Or, as Farrer himself states in his introduction to Leibniz's *Theodicy*, God's mind "is not, of course, discursive; he does not successively turn over the leaves of an infinite book of sample worlds, for then he would never come to the end of it. Embracing infinite possibility in the single act of his mind he settles his will with intuitive immediacy upon the best."[60] The question why this world instead of another "is one which we neither need to ask nor indeed are able to ask."[61] We are to face the world as we find it, and engage it, flaws and all. In any case, Farrer states, "I can no more think myself out of this world than I can jump off my own shadow."[62]

God's creation of the world as it is allows both the freedom of human will and the possibility of evil. Freedom of human will is necessary for the human capacity to love, including love of the divine. God could have created a world of machines or puppets instead of creating humanity with free will. The Creator could have "thought to glorify himself by constructing a cosmic gramophone, streamlined for the production of symphonic Alleluias."[63] Instead, it was God's desire "to create beings able to know and to love him."[64] Love is impossible without freedom and the capacity to choose, but freedom also allows the possibility of evil human choices. Without freedom to choose badly, there would be no freedom to choose well, or to love God.

Providence

Providence means "foreseeing care," and God's providence "must always be seen as the accompaniment, or the instrument, of more definite aims," the first of which would be "creation and preservation."[65] Farrer states that God's providence acts upon the world as it exists "for continued creation and conservation, and in furtherance of redemption."[66] God's works "are not irrational, they are endlessly intelligible; but that means there is always more and more for us to understand in them." We may trust that God's providences will work the natural action of things into "higher designs," although "we have seldom any reason to trust our guesses as to what these higher designs may be."[67] God "works everything into his further purposes, for his work never ceases; and he always goes on from the actual situation into which things have come."[68] Providence is the function of salvation: "Those of God's creatures which are salvable, he saves."[69] Providence is active and ongoing in all contexts, whether or not we understand it.

Providence is "an aspect of creation itself," as creation itself was "not finished in six days" but is "perpetually proceeding." To illustrate this, Farrer points out that we are all "in process of being created." Farrer had many opportunities to experience that truth as a teacher of undergraduates in college at Oxford. He asks, relative to young people, "Who knows the person each will finally become?" With a touch of humor, he adds that "even those whom the eyes of youth see as set, finished and irredeemable are not all such fossils either." Not including himself among the fossils, Farrer quips, "Do you think these pages I am here composing are the playing over of an old record?" On the contrary, he states, making what seems to be an autobiographical comment, the "author becomes a different thinker by thinking his way through his paragraphs," and it is "in ourselves that we best see the operation of such mysteries."[70] In perhaps a similar way, Farrer notes that St. John "was not the same man" after writing the book of Revelation "as he had been before."[71] St. John was recreated in the inspired process of creating.

Providence does not magically remove the obstacles and burdens of our life, but providence is actively present with us in the midst of all our contexts and challenges. Our facing the evils and flaws of the world also points us to an appreciation of God's action or providence. Farrer admits it is "natural" for us to hope for divine providence in terms of God's acting as we would if we could, "by altering what we see before us, perhaps removing an obstacle, perhaps mending a bridge." But that is not the usual way of providence. Jesus at Gethsemane prayed for removal of the passion, but the divine will "brought the new life of resurrection out of it" instead of removing it. We are likely to experience divine providence in a similar way. According to Farrer, "God's supreme skill lies not in manipulation of the existing level, but in drawing some new thing out of existent states of affairs." Farrer allows for the possibility of a more direct intervention but states that "when God removes evils in the human sort of way, it is commonly by the employment of human hands."[72] Providence can work through us, but it is not magic, and it will seldom mean an easy escape from the challenges of our life.

God's own "divine way is to make unthought-of goods out of permitted evils and to triumph by new creation."[73] The "supreme prerogative of the divine art," Farrer notes, "is to draw good even from evil."[74] Indeed, "God can use and does use for his glory everything that happens, however unhelpful it seems, where people trust him."[75] Providence continues active through all the events of daily life, and it may work in surprising ways with unexpected material, drawing the raw material of disasters and failures into higher designs. Brian Hebblethwaite states that for Farrer, "God's infinite contrivance draws some good out of every cross-accident." But God "has not calculated the accident with a view to the resultant good."[76] Instead of interpreting every evil as a part of a divine plan, we should see every evil as an occasion for God's providence.

Farrer offers a most hopeful understanding of divine providence. Perhaps the most significant lesson regarding evil, according to Farrer, is that "the saving power of God" can bring the best out of the worst.[77] That is the lesson of the cross. God's creative work "never ceases," and "there is always something his Providence does, even for the most tragically stricken." Similarly, Farrer states that "there is always a will of God to be sought in any situation, however unpromising—to be sought by our minds, that it may be saved by our hands."[78] With God, no situation is ultimately lost.

In light of Farrer's hopeful theology of divine providence in the worst situations, his understanding of the condition relative to God of "imbeciles"(as the mentally impaired were labeled in Farrer's time) or those with other forms of "idiocy" is strikingly disappointing and inconsistent with his other positions. In an appendix to *Love Almighty and Ills Unlimited* titled "Imperfect Lives," he states that "one of the commonly reckoned evils of human life is the death of speechless infants, before they reach the stature of humanity; another is the survival of imbeciles, who are incapable of ever attaining it." He adds that "it is an accident common to organic existence that weak, puny, and imperfect examples of any given species should sometimes be produced," but the "theological problem specially posed by these disorders" is that "we do not know how we should relate to the mercy of God beings who never enjoy a glimmer of reason."[79] Farrer holds a rather constricted view of divine mercy in this context.

For Farrer, the question is whether such people are "capable of eternal salvation, or are they not?" He concludes that "the rational person is not there" and that, "if it is an amiable absurdity in us to pity his non-existence, we should not suppose him to be the object of an all-wise Compassion."[80] Similarly, and unfortunately, in *Finite and Infinite,* Farrer asserts that "eccentricity, stupidity, mania, deficiency, idiocy are various privations" of the proper character of human normality. But, he concludes, "whether an idiot is to be called a man or not is an unprofitable question; he is a man so spoilt or diminished that one may hesitate to apply the name."[81] This represents a curiously dark understanding of the divine and merciful providence that is constantly active and creatively present for even the most tragically stricken.

Ann Loades has suggested that these statements by Farrer may reflect his frustrations with the limited capacities of his own daughter, Caroline.[82] Curtis also mentions Caroline's situation relative to *Love Almighty and Ills Unlimited* and states that "experience, not theory alone, underlies that book."[83] It seems incredible and indeed cold blooded that Farrer would hesitate to affirm the humanity of a disabled person on the basis of "privations" such as eccentricity and stupidity.

Nevertheless, Farrer does present a thorough treatment of the problem of evil in light of philosophical theology and the realities of living faith. The problem of evil, of course, remains a mystery of faith. But it is a mystery we share in the company of Christ. Farrer uses the story of a woman in the pain of childbirth who is not comforted by her doctor's explanation that "the pain of human childbirth is the price of man's nobility." It still hurts. But she is filled with joy and forgets her pain when she sees her newborn son. Drawing out the analogy, Farrer states that "God does not give us explanations; he gives up a Son." The Son "is better than an explanation" because "the explanation of our death leaves us no less dead than we were," but the Son "gives us a life, in which to live."[84] The only real answer to the problem of evil is relational. The Son gives life and stands with us, even in the face of evil.

No one should turn away from God because of evil in the world, because "the severity of the diseases we endure is a poor argument to refuse the remedy." In "The Trinity in Whom We Live," originally given as a radio address on Trinity Sunday, Farrer states that Christians face evils in the world like everyone else, and "we neither deny nor palliate any of these evils, for we do not . . . uphold a theology of divine benevolence or pretend that the kingdom of God is an omnipotent welfare state." Christians can not "claim that God has made us able to explain or justify the evil of our condition: we claim that he has taken measures to save us from the wreck. Himself bearing our pains, and crucified for our salvation, he has lifted us into the love of the Blessed Trinity."[85] God does not rescue us from evil in a magical way or divert evil from us, but God is with us in the midst of evil and draws us into the higher designs of divine love.

Loades concludes her essay "Austin Farrer on *Love Almighty*" by stating that "the incarnation is the means by which God brings good out of blackest evil and loves and saves whatever there is to be loved and saved."[86] In *Lord I Believe*, Farrer states that Jesus "consented to die" in the garden at Gethsemane when he "prayed the prayer of nature, asking to live," and found it unprayable. "Then the Lord's Prayer became the flesh and blood of the Lord who gave it."[87] Jesus embraces the human encounter with evil in obedience to God's will and shares the victory of the cross to fulfill God's kingdom by giving himself. Jesus lives out the divine response to the problem of evil in human terms by obedience, personal presence, relationship, generosity, and sacrifice.

Farrer likewise urges us to pray in the face of evil. He notes that in the Lord's Prayer we are called on by Jesus to pray "that we may not be brought into temptation, but rescued from the wicked fiend." And "it is by so praying, and by so trusting, that we allow God the victory over his enemy, and give occasion to that divine miracle, and masterpiece of wonders, which brings out of evils permitted a good designed, and out of death life immortal."[88]

In the last paragraph of *Finite and Infinite*, Farrer states that "as I wrote this, the German armies were occupying Paris, after a campaign prodigal of blood and human distress." In this tragic context, it was not possible for rational theology to tell "whether this has or has not been an unqualified and irretrievable disaster to mankind and especially to the men who died." But, Farrer asserts, "it is another matter, if we believe that God Incarnate also died, and rose from the dead." Rational theology "knows only that whether Paris stands or falls, whether men die or live, God is God, and so long as any spiritual creature survives, God is to be adored."[89] Even in the face of evil it is possible to pray and, in praying, to share Christ's suffering and victory.

5

Transforming Images

Christians must "listen to the Spirit speaking divine things," and this is done as we "quicken our own minds with the life of the inspired images." In *The Glass of Vision,* Farrer notes that he has "heard it wisely said that in Scripture there is not a line of theology, and of philosophy not so much as an echo." The task of theology is "the analysis and criticism of the revealed images," but theology "tests and determines the sense of the images, it does not create it." It will not do to join the medieval scholastics in "the hunt for theological propositions" from which a "correct system of doctrine" may be "deduced by logical method." This approach will "close our ears to the voice of Scripture." Similarly, Farrer warns that the "modern tendency" to "seek after historical record" can fail to disclose "either the voice of God, or the substance of supernatural mystery."[1] Farrer upholds the essential role of images in living and understanding Christian faith.

In the opening chapter of *A Rebirth of Images,* Farrer notes that "the human imagination has always been controlled by certain basic images, in which man's own nature, his relation to his fellows, and his dependence upon the divine power find expression." These images are absorbed from the individual's society, "partly through the suggestion of outward acts and the significance of words, partly, it would seem, by some more hidden means of appropriation," so that "the contents of other people's minds flow into ours at a sub-conscious level, even across gaps in time and space." In this way, "ancestral images" may "be carried and communicated to the next generation by those who are unaware of their existence at the conscious level."[2] There are times when a writer may "have an idea or an image in his mind effectively enough to shape what he says, without his being aware of it at all."[3] Images are formative for human imagination, understanding, perspective, and communication.

Farrer's belief in the role of ancestral images and the unconscious is close to Carl G. Jung's understanding of the human unconscious "as an objective and collective psyche."[4] In *Symbols of Transformation,* Jung explains that creative fantasy "draws upon the forgotten and long buried primitive mind with its host of images, which are to be found in the mythologies of all ages and all peoples," and that "the sum of these images constitutes the collective unconscious, a heritage which is potentially present in every individual."[5] A person who seeks to live without myth or outside it, Jung argues, "is like one uprooted, having no true link either with the past, or with the ancestral life which continues within him, or yet with human society."[6] He also warns that "we have forgotten the age-old fact that God speaks chiefly through dreams and visions."[7] For Jung, "irrational factors" (such as the images of the collective unconscious) "play the largest, indeed the decisive, role in all processes of psychic transformation."[8] For Farrer, these ancient ancestral images may likewise be found in a collective or social unconscious and play a decisive role for all processes of transformation in faith.

Farrer's approach may also be related to Travis Du Priest's understanding of knowing the Holy Spirit through image and metaphor. Du Priest states that to embrace and be embraced by the Spirit as churches and communities of faith, "we must turn to the collective imagery and metaphors of poetry, fable, mythology, legend, folklore, story, art, music, architecture, sculpture—the world of graphic and verbal metaphor." This is "a world of symbol that transports us from one realm to another," a "world largely outside of rational analysis and comprehension." Du Priest states that the Spirit "nourishes us anywhere she can rise to consciousness through image and metaphor, even in archaic and ancient tales and symbolic myths."[9] The Spirit engages and shapes our lives through images.

Farrer states that humanity cannot conceive the ineffable "except in images," and these images must be "divinely given" for humanity "to know a supernatural divine act."[10] The "formation of the images" responds to "the supernatural action of God," so that "in the case of divine inspiration . . . the inspired mind projects images."[11] The images are "supernaturally formed, and supernaturally made intelligible to faith." It is "what the images signify" that faith discerns, but "we cannot discern it except *through* the images." Farrer warns that "we cannot by-pass the images to seize an imageless truth."[12]

Rodger Forsman explains that, for Farrer, "the Scriptures are essentially a tissue of images interwoven with historical and other kinds of literary material" and that the images "carry the weight of revelation." Farrer's "key insight is that images are inspired because they are salvific, i.e. enable us to engage in saving activity."[13] Ingolf Dalferth states that Farrer was interested in the "working" of the imagination of evangelists such as John, Matthew, and Mark because "he believed their imagination to be the locus of divine inspiration and revelation; and for the same reason he was interested in the literary pattern of the biblical texts because he believed them to be the sole guide to their writers' imagination and hence to God's revelation."[14] Stephen Platten notes that "figural imagination" was "perhaps the single greatest influence on Farrer and his spirituality, as seen through his sermons and as glimpsed through his speculative theology."[15] With respect to the importance of images for Farrer, Platten states that Farrer's mind was "permeated with poetic sensibility." His love for poetry was reinforced by his Oxford acquaintances, including "literary personalities" he met as a member of the undergraduate Oxford University Socratic Society, such as Elizabeth Jennings, Anne Ridler, Dorothy Sayers, Charles Williams, Neville Coghill, Hugo Dyson, J. R. R. Tolkien, and C. S. Lewis.[16]

Farrer's understanding of the necessity for images of faith is close to that of Dorothy Sayers, who states in *The Mind of the Maker* that "to forbid the making of [verbal] pictures about God would be to forbid thinking about God at all, for man is so made that he has no way to think except in pictures."[17] Sayers recalls the commandment against making graven images (idols) but states that "no legislation could prevent the making of verbal pictures" of God who "walks in the garden," and who "stretches out His arm," and whose "voice shakes the cedars."[18] Farrer explains that "the rejection of idolatry meant not the destruction but the liberation of the images," and that "nowhere are the images in more vigour than in the Old Testament, where they speak of God but are not he."[19] Images are at the heart of the divine-human relation.

Spiritual power is found in the images of faith. Christ actually lived the images of faith he received from Jewish tradition. He "was himself Israel, and appointed twelve men to be his typical 'sons.' He applied to himself the prophecies of a redemptive suffering for mankind attributed to Israel by Isaiah and Jewish tradition." Similarly, Christ "displayed, in the action of the supper, the infinitely complex and fertile image of sacrifice and communion, of expiation and covenant." Farrer notes that "these tremendous images, and others like them, are not the whole of Christ's teaching, but they set forth the supernatural mystery which is the heart of the teaching." Without them, the teaching would be "instruction in piety and morals," not supernatural revelation.[20]

The biblical images are powerful: they "thunder and lighten in the prophetic oracles." For Farrer, "it is the covenant, the word, the divine kingship, the session on the mercy-seat, that burst forth with threatening, persuasion and hope, by way of reaction to the abominations of Israelite apostasy and the movements of Chaldaean conquest."[21] The image on the page of scripture, "taken as it stands," has "life-giving power in it." That power will be discovered by the "Bible-reader," who "will immerse himself in the single image on the page before him"—unlike the theologian, who "may confuse the images," and the metaphysician, who "may speculate about them."[22] In this way, the motions of the Bible reader's soul (such as gratitude for the amazing gift of a share in the unique divine sonship, awe at the thought of being possessed by the Spirit of God, or sorrow for the darkness that veils what is now seen in the clarity of faith) "take place within the field of the image."[23] Images allow expression of faith's depth and intensity.

With respect to divine revelation and moving the minds of St. Paul or St. John (or anyone else), Farrer admits that the process is "a profound and invisible mystery." But if we observe "the perceptible process in the inspired mind, the psychological fact, then we may say that it is a process of images which live as it were by their own life and impose themselves with authority." These images "demand to be thought in this way or that, and not otherwise."[24] For example, concerning the "veil" between God and humanity, Farrer declares that it is not "blank," no matter how "impenetrable" it may seem. The veil "is painted with the image of God, and God himself painted it, and made it indelible with his blood, when he was nailed to it for us men and for our salvation." God is thereby known "through the image, and by faith."[25] We may know God through the definitive image of the cross.

Farrer underscores the importance of biblical images by considering whether —and if so, how—the doctrine of the Trinity is in the New Testament. He considers several methods, but he does not find all methods helpful. He notes the "new scholastic way," using statistics and lexicography to count ("painfully") and classify the texts of St. Paul or St. John in which the persons of the Trinity "are mentioned, either severally or in connexion with one another." This, Farrer explains, is "the method of the research-degree thesis," but in this case it is "false in its assumptions and inconclusive in its results." The problem is that the method assumes St. Paul or St. John to be a systematic theologian, though a "very unsystematic systematic theologian, no doubt, too impulsive and enthusiastic to put his material in proper order or to standardize his terminology." However, this problem can be remedied by "anyone who has a decent modern education," Farrer observes with wry humor, and the student of this method "will be rewarded a research degree for doing it."[26]

But, Farrer counters, what if there were "no system coming to birth in the apostle's mind at all—not, that is, on the conceptual level?" Suppose that the apostle's "thought centred round a number of vital images, which lived with the life of images, not of concepts." In this case, each image has "its own conceptual conventions, proper to the figure it embodies," and "a single over-all conceptual analysis will be about as useful for the interpretation of the Apostle's writings as a bulldozer for the cultivation of a miniature landscape-garden." Farrer states that the various images do indeed "attract one another and tend to fuse" in the apostle's mind, "but they have their own way of doing this, according to their own imagery laws, and not according to the principles of conceptual system."[27] With this example, Farrer presents the essential place of images and their interpretation for understanding revelation. "The images, of themselves, signify and reveal."[28] Images are living things for Farrer, the very "stuff" of inspiration and revelation.[29]

The "God-given images lived, not statically, but with an inexpressible creative force" in the apostolic mind.[30] In the apostolic era, Farrer states, "the several distinct images grew together into fresh unities, opened out in new detail, attracted to themselves and assimilated further image-material: all this within the life of a generation. This is the way inspiration worked."[31] Farrer's description of this dynamic process of inspiration through converging images recalls Dorothy Emmet's statement regarding religious imagery: "A symbolic phrase may gather up into itself different strands of meaning and transmute them into a new unity, in which all these strands may be woven together."[32]

According to Farrer, divine truth is "supernaturally communicated" in "an act of inspired thinking which falls into the shape of certain images."[33] The prophets "were under the pressure of supernatural mysteries speaking through living images." Likewise, "through the secret act of God by which the apostles were inspired there came upon us in imaged presentation the shape of the mystery of our redemption." As the minds of the apostles were "possessed and moulded" by this imaged presentation, "it possesses and moulds ours," so that "we are taken up into the movement of the life above all creatures."[34]

With respect to the scriptures, Farrer acknowledges that the "decisive shaping of the images" may have taken place elsewhere. But we may "rightly suppose that the dominant images of the New Testament were the common property of the teaching Church." Indeed these images are "still alive and moving in the writers' minds," so that they "continue to enter into fresh combinations, to elaborate themselves, to beget new applications."[35] But the integrity of the images themselves must be respected in interpretation. They are "distinct images" and "must be interpreted according to their own laws." The images must not be forced "to the pattern of one another."[36]

Image and Event

We cannot separate the images of the New Testament from the historical record it contains. The "inspired image and historical memory are so fused" in the Gospel of Mark, Farrer states, that "it is virtually impossible to pull them apart." The "great images interpreted the events of Christ's ministry, death and resurrection, and the events interpreted the images; the interplay of the two is revelation." Event and image are correlative for Farrer, so that "the events without the image would be no revelation at all, and the images without the events would remain shadows on the clouds."[37] The events, standing alone, "are not revelation, for they do not by themselves reveal the divine work which is accomplished in them." For example, "the martyrdom of a virtuous Rabbi and his miraculous return are not of them-selves the redemption of the world."[38] But the interplay of image and event can convey the revelatory power of Jesus's life, death, and resurrection.

The "interplay of image and event" likewise continues in the lives of the apos-tles: "As the divine action continues to unfold its character in the descent of the Spirit, in the apostolic mission, and in the mystical fellowship, so the images given by Christ continue to unfold within the apostolic mind, in such fashion as to reveal the nature of the supernatural existence of the apostolic church."[39] These images continue to be formative as their meanings unfold for generations of Christians.

Inspiration, Revelation, and Image

The images of faith continue to live, inspire, and influence as the life of the church continues. Farrer states that as we read the text of St. Paul's writing, we may "sud-denly perceive that the apostle's feet have gone through the floor and his head through the roof, and that he is speaking in the large dimension of inspired vision." Accordingly, "in the authority and the spirit of a great image," St. Paul "returns to settle the matter in hand."[40] Inspiration, revelation, and image are deeply con-nected for Farrer. He offers a fascinating image of his own in this regard, stating that if the authors of the scripture were "capable of inspired thinking," they did it "with their pens in their hands."[41]

Images of the Trinity in the scriptures are of particular interest to Farrer. His method for tracing their development is to look for it as "a particular image," to "isolate it and distinguish it from other images," and then "to ask what place it occupies in the world of New Testament images—whether dominant or subordi-nate, vital or inessential: and how other images are affected by it." Then, "if we like," it is possible "to ask what metaphysical comment the New Testament image of the Trinity provokes, and which subsequent theological conceptualizations do least violence to it."[42] At the outset of his search for this image, Farrer reaches back to Isaiah 11, "in which we read of an anointed king, whose anointing is not with oil, but with the Spirit of the Lord, resting sevenfold upon him." Farrer concludes that "here are the elements of the Trinitarian image."[43]

Farrer then references the Testaments of the XII Patriarchs, which he describes as a "famous Jewish writing, known to the principal New Testament authors." In this "we may take as the next step forward a text which overlays the idea of spiri-tual anointing with the idea of divine sonship." The heavens will be opened for a "supreme anointed head," and the "hallowing" (identified as the Holy Spirit) will descend upon him "with the Father's voice as from Abraham to Isaac." Farrer observes that "'the Father's voice as from Abraham to Isaac' is the voice of the Father upraised in blessing upon an only and beloved Son," which is identified with "the unforgettable and repeated designation of Isaac in the most memorable history about him."[44]

Farrer then continues to trace the developing image into the New Testament, where we may now see "the whole image become fact in the baptism of Jesus Christ." He points to the Gospel of Mark (1:9–11), in which "the heavens are now opened indeed, the voice of the Father audibly designates a divine Isaac as his beloved Son, and the spirit of hallowing descends visibly as a dove." For Mark, the historical event of Jesus's baptism is "the temporal manifestation of a state of things older than the world," although Mark is not "explicit in his trinitarian image."[45]

Further development of the Trinitarian image is evident in the Gospel of John, which "sets forth the image of the Trinity as representing the mystery of divine love into which we are taken up." For John, the Son was clearly "Son before the world began." The Son is seen in John's Revelation "like a Lamb standing as slaughtered, having seven horns and seven eyes, which are the seven spirits of God." Farrer states that these "are the Holy Ghost, manifested as sevenfold vision and sevenfold strength." He likewise identifies "a plain allusion in the wording of the vision to Isaiah's oracle on the prince endowed sevenfold with the Spirit of the Lord."[46]

St. John also describes "the same sevenfold Spirit of God as a cluster of seven flames burning before the Father's throne." With respect to this image, the "sevenfold light of the Holy Ghost burns before the Father's majesty," blazing in the eyes of the mystical Lamb, and the "Father's sevenfold plenitude of Spirit is bestowed upon the Son." According to Farrer, "St. John is content to set forth the image," although John "does not speculatively determine the relation of the Son to the Father." That would come later, with the development of theology. Instead, "we have in St. John simply the *image* of the Father, Son and Spirit, placed by relation to us and our salvation in the transcendent place he assigns it."[47] In powerful ways, and sometimes in fantastic ways, Farrer discerns the biblical image of the Trinity.

The Interplay and Relation of Images

The scriptural images have integrity and meaning that are proper to themselves, but the images may be related to one another in terms of "master-images and subordinate images."[48] Farrer states that "in the prophets, as in the apostles, we must distinguish between the master-images for which there are no equivalents, and the subordinate images by which the master-images are set forth or brought to bear."[49] However, it is "an impossibility" for either prophets or apostles to be "inspired to devise simply new master-images." Instead, revelation grows "only through images already implanted." These master-images are transformed as they grow, and in growing, "they throw out fresh branches, they fertilize neighbouring and as yet purely natural imaginations."[50]

Farrer states that "within the field of revealed truth, the principal images provide a canon to the lesser images." For example, in the Gospel of John, the image of Christ's judging is reduced to that of his coming: "The light has only to come into the world, and it shows up the dark patches: and men's judgment is effected by their turning their back on the candle of the world." But, Farrer states, judgment has not been disposed of, even when "judgment is thus reduced to advent." Judgment remains as an additional truth to the truth of the advent vision, "though now subordinated to it."[51] St. John "reduces" the subordinate images "to terms of others," but the subordinate images "no more disappear or lose their force, than do the whole body of images, when we remember that they are no more than images, and so reduce them to the one ineffable simplicity of God's saving love."[52]

The "play of secondary images and ideas under the pressure of the great images" may also be seen in the Gospel of Mark, where, for example, texts about the boy in the garden, Jesus's shrouding by Joseph, and the boy in the tomb are held together by "verbal echoes" and "by the name of Joseph." Farrer states that "no one's salvation depends on the comparison between Joseph with his eleven false brethren and Jesus with his eleven cowardly disciples: or on the antique symbolism of the robe of honor." But the "substance of the truth is in the great images which lie behind" the secondary images. Primary images such as the figure of the Son of Man, the ceremony of the sacramental body, the bloody sacrifice of the Lamb, and the enthronement of the Lord's Anointed lie behind the Marcan secondary images, and it is "through the secondary images," Farrer states, that "the force of the primary images is felt.[53]

One image may also help us to understand another image. For example, Farrer considers the light shed by the image of "Christ as the Word through whom God made the worlds" on the image of the Trinity, even though the Word image and other images are "not of themselves Trinitarian at all." However, he cautions that in comparing these images, we must "remember that they are distinct images" and "not force them to the pattern of one another." The biblical images have their own integrity that must not be violated. Otherwise, we—like the church fathers—will fail to "respect the method of images" and inevitably "force and confuse the sense of scripture." Farrer concludes that the divine Son is the "eternal and adequate recipient" of the eternally bestowed Spirit, according to the Trinitarian images of St. Mark and St. John.[54]

Farrer's understanding of primary and secondary images may be related to John Macquarrie's discussion of John 1:18 in *Jesus Christ in Modern Thought,* in which Macquarrie states that the "theme of life, more-than-natural life, expressed in the words and deeds of Jesus, runs through all that range of metaphors which are applied to him." For example, Macquarrie notes that "the water which the Samaritan woman drew from the well originally dug by Jacob becomes a symbol of the living water of Christ, and he is likewise the living bread and the light of the world and the true vine (contrasted with the vine that symbolized Israel) and the good shepherd (contrasted with the hirelings and false prophets)."[55] The primary image of life in Christ may be seen in a variety of secondary images.

Development and Transformation of Images

One of the most fascinating aspects of Farrer's understanding of images concerns their development and transformation. The images have their own integrity, but they also may undergo change. Farrer urges that Christ transformed the fundamental images of faith in Judaism "by clothing himself in them and dying in the armour." He contrasts the Old Testament prophets and the Christian apostles relative to these images, noting that there was "a crisis of images in the experience of the witnesses to the incarnation" unlike anything experienced by the prophets, who for the most part saw themselves "as pure traditionalists, appealing over the head of a degenerate and paganized monarchy back to Moses and David."[56] But the Christian apostles could not be pure Jewish traditionalists, and the images of Judaism were not sufficient for a new faith.

The prophets were "not publishing a new religion." The images of faith were taken for granted by the prophets, and "the particular warnings and pleadings of God" were prophetically revealed on the basis of the images. But the apostles were publishing a new religion, and in them the "great images of faith" were "freshly minted and reborn through Christ's incarnation."[57] A transformed faith called for a transformation of images, and a Christian "rebirth of images" (as Farrer titles one of his books on St. John's Revelation) was necessary. Farrer states that "religion is transformed when the images are transformed, and their transformation will determine the character of spirituality." The transformation of images is seen in the birth of Christianity, which "is a visible rebirth of images."[58]

This is not to say, however, that the images of faith were unaltered relative to the prophets. Farrer explains that "the fundamental images are being continually and imperceptibly reinterpreted in the direction of a supernatural sense, even though the prophets themselves do not know it." In this regard, "God must make a *new* covenant, he must circumcise the *heart,* he must raise up a *new* David, the earthly vessel of heavenly grace must be made worthy of it; not by itself, but by grace."[59] For Farrer, the great images of faith "themselves are undergoing change in the prophets" by a "supernatural act" that is "the process of the incarnation of God preparing its own way and casting its shadow before." For example, Farrer states, "the true temple will have to be no temple, but the flesh of the Virgin's Child" because "nothing merely natural will ever be able to embody it."[60]

The images of faith, the "old archetypes," were "already half transformed under the leading of God in the expectant faith of Israel." These images of faith were then put on by Christ and "further transformed by what Christ suffered and did when he put them on." They were transformed "by their all being combined in his one person." With respect to this combination and transformation of images in Christ, Farrer asks, "What sort of victorious David can it be, who is also the martyred Israel and the Lamb of sacrifice? What sort of new Adam can it be, who is also the temple of God? And what sort of living temple can it be, who is also the Word of God whereby the world was made?" The "choice, use and combination of images made by Christ and the Spirit must be simply a supernatural work," Farrer concludes.[61] These images of faith are, in fact, a divine gift.

The rebirthing of images reflects and continues a process that was at the heart of Jesus's ministry. Farrer states that "Jesus did not sweep away the elaborated forms of Judaism; He fused them into a new unity and created them afresh." And the Epistles and Gospels provide "a continuation of the creative fusion which had its place in the mind and very existence of Jesus, in whom the old was born again from on high."[62] The divine work and process of giving images was also "continued by the Spirit of Christ moving the minds of the Apostles."[63]

The divine giving of images to the apostles was not a heavenly dictation but a process in which the apostolic minds "performed a supernatural act" as they "developed and understood the images of faith." Farrer states that supernatural acts "are continuous with natural functions, of which they are, so to speak, the upward prolongations." The boundary between natural and supernatural in this process "need be neither objectively evident nor subjectively felt." In this sense, grace may perfect, or complete, nature seamlessly. Farrer states that the apostle developing the images of faith "would find himself to be performing a sort of activity well-known to the Rabbinic Jew, the activity of seeking fresh insights by the comparison and fusion of sacred image." But now the figures of Christ's self-revelation provide the center point for the images, and the desired insights concern Christ and his saving work.[64]

Farrer states that "we must regard the Christian revolution as essentially a transformation of images." The images in Judaism of "Joseph the saint of sacrificial loving kindness, the ritual Lamb of the atonement, David the viceroy of God, the word of God's presence and power, Israel the Son of God, [and] Adam the new-created Image of God" were all "reborn in one divine Saviour out of the sepulchre of Christ."[65] Also in Christ were fused the images of "heroic and unmerited suffering for God's glory and the good of the brethren, especially in the figure of Joseph," which was itself "tending to fuse with that of the blood-offering in atonement of sin"; the "image of the Messiah, in whose enthronement the Kingdom of God would be manifested on earth"; "images of the divine power and presence —God is in heaven, but his 'Name' is in the temple, his Wisdom or Word or Spirit is in the mind of the prophet, or, in some degree, wherever there is a mind alive with the divine law"; and "an image of divine sonship, belonging primarily to the chosen people."[66] A host of Old Testament images are reborn and fulfilled in Christ.

The rebirth of images may be studied throughout the New Testament, but in the book of Revelation, more than anywhere else, it is possible to go deeper into the "heart of the process." "Nowhere else" is there a writing "so simply devoted to the liberation of images." Farrer states that the evangelists are restricted by the "historical actuality upon which they fit" the images, and the New Testament Epistles express the images "only in so far as serves the purpose of instruction or exhortation," but Revelation "writes of heaven and things to come, that is, of a realm which has no shape at all but that which the images give it." This allows the image to "grow to the fullness of its inborn nature, like a tree in a wide meadow."[67]

For example, Farrer notes in *A Rebirth of Images* that "when St. John's spirit flies up through the door of heaven, he sees a Lamb, standing as slaughtered: a symbol as pregnant for the new faith as that which Moses saw in the old, the flame of a bush, burning unconsumed."[68] He also states that "wherever the sacrificial Lamb is mentioned by Christians, the lamb or ram which God himself provided to redeem Isaac is not long out of mind." He compares Abraham's assurance (though "not knowing how, and at his wits' end") to Isaac that God will provide a lamb of offering and "the pathos of St John's vision" as he weeps because none is found worthy to open the heavenly book and loose its seals. In both instances, uncertainty and dismay do not last. John finds more than a ram or lamb in a thicket. One of the elders says to him, "Weep not: behold, the Lion that is of the Tribe of Judah, the Root of David, hath prevailed to open the book and the seven seals thereof." And in the midst of the throne and the four cherubim, he sees "a Lamb standing as slaughtered, having seven horns and seven eyes."[69]

In *A Rebirth of Images,* Farrer gives another example of rebirthing an Old Testament image in the book of Revelation, this one concerning the atonement in blood of Leviticus 17:11: "'The soul of all flesh is the blood thereof, and I have given it to you upon the altar to make atonement for your souls: for the blood thereof shall make atonement instead of the soul.'" He also refers to Leviticus 17:14, which states that the blood is the life of every creature. Mindful of the image of blood atonement, Farrer turns to Revelation and states that "the lives of the martyrs are offered as atoning sacrifices" and that St. John understands their deaths "as meritorious and atoning, and as giving force to their prayers." The "merit and atoning force" of the deaths of the martyrs are "grounded in the work of Christ."[70]

Farrer refers to the Lamb standing as slaughtered in Revelation 5, the slaughtered saints in Revelation 6, and the description in Revelation 12:11 of those who "'overcame (the dragon) because of the blood of the Lamb and because of the word of their testimony and for that they loved not their life, even to the death.'"

Farrer notes that "the blood of Christ both atones and cries, uttering better words than Abel's." The blood of the martyrs also cries "for the extirpation of the race of Cain," and the slaughtered saints are the "'firstfruits,' waiting for the fulfilment of the harvest of souls, the Pentecost when their number will be accomplished and their cry heard." Christ is the "firstfruit" of the slaughtered saints, and "they are the firstfruits of the Church. Presently the whole harvest of martyrs will be gathered in: and then the harvest-home."[71] In all these ways, the Levitical image of blood atonement is reborn in the sacrifice of Christ and the saints, which is the blood of the Lamb and the martyrs described in Revelation.[72]

Farrer continues the "method and approach" to Revelation of *A Rebirth of Images* (though with "greatly" altered details of exposition) in *The Revelation of St. John the Divine*.[73] For example, he considers the image of the Lion of Judah, who is worthy to open the scroll sealed with seven seals (Revelation 5). But the Lion "paradoxically appears in the guise of a Lamb slaughtered (that is, with his throat cut) yet standing on his feet." For Farrer, the "sudden appearance of the saving [L]amb in the hour of need" must "recall the sudden appearance of the ram which redeemed Isaac (Gen. xxii. 13)." This lamb, provided by God to redeem Abraham's only son, "is a type of the beloved Son whom God spares not to give." The Lamb of God is "the victim who lives, yet who, unlike Isaac, was really offered, bound to the wood."[74] Once again, the image of the ram in the thicket that saves Isaac is reborn in the sacrifice of the Lamb, God's own Son, who dies on the cross for human salvation.

Farrer's original, brilliant, and perhaps idiosyncratic tendencies may be seen in images identified by him in *The Revelation of St. John the Divine*. For example, with respect to the seven angels who blow trumpets after the Lamb opens the seventh seal (Revelation 8), Farrer notes it is "obvious" that "St. John's trumpets are Michael's trumpet expanded into a sevenfold series" and that a yearly trumpet that "both announces a new era and prepares for the Great Day (Atonement) is an obvious symbol for the trumpet of Michael (Isa. xxvii. 13, I Thess. iv. 16–17, Matt. xxiv. 31)." According to Farrer, "Michael's trumpet is basically a trumpet of assembly and of release (Num. x. 2, Lev. xxv. 9)," and "it becomes a trumpet of resurrection" since "most of those it summons are in the grave."[75] Farrer's conclusions illustrate the process of rebirthing Old Testament images in a way that may prove fascinating—if occasionally doubtful—for many readers.

With respect to the heavenly Jerusalem that descends from God and lies foursquare (Revelation 21), Farrer states:

> What can St. John mean by saying that the city's height is equal to her length and breadth? Perhaps it is most reasonable to see the height as that of a great acropolis, crowned with walls. St. John no doubt wants the cube for its own sake. It is a shape mathematically perfect, like the sphere; it symbolizes, as we have

explained, the completeness of the number of the elect; it is the form of the Holy
of Holies (I Kings vi. 20) and as such appears as the central feature of Ezekiel's
city (Ezek. xli. 4).[76]

The images of Solomon's temple and Ezekiel's vision of the New Temple are thus
reborn and fulfilled in the heavenly Jerusalem of Revelation, a reborn image. In
a similar way, a fourfold literary image of the heavenly Jerusalem is provided by
the English poet William Blake: "The Four Living Creatures Chariots of Humanity Divine Incomprehensible / In beautiful Paradises expand These are the Four
Rivers of Paradise / And the Four Faces of Humanity fronting the Four Cardinal
Points / Of Heaven going forward forward irresistible from Eternity to Eternity."[77]

Hieromonk Alexander Golitzin likewise states that "John the Seer's cubical
New Jerusalem" is "unmistakably derived from the dimensions of the Holy of
Holies (cf. 1 Kgs. 6:20). That point on earth where, as in the vision of Isaiah (Isa.
6:1–6), heaven and Earth coalesce becomes in the Revelation the new creation
itself, where God and the Lamb are to be immediately and everywhere present."[78]
A heavenly image from the Old Testament is transformed and made new in Revelation.

New Testament images can also be reborn. Farrer uses the Gospel of Luke to
consider the "dovetailed revelations" to Zechariah and to Mary, "not only in respect
of the supernaturality of what is promised them, but also in respect of their degree
of faith." Farrer perceives "a close parallelism between the two annunciation-
stories." Both Zechariah and Mary ask the angel Gabriel how these unexpected
births are to occur. Zechariah states that he and his wife are old; Mary says that
she is a virgin. Zechariah's disbelief is avenged by "temporary dumbness," but
"Mary has the opportunity of a second answer, denied to Zacharias by his dumbness; she makes her submission. 'Behold the handmaid of the Lord; be it to me
according to thy word.'"[79]

Farrer continues his literary analysis of the "dovetailed" images, noting that
"single visions are of no certain authority; independent visions, mutually confirm-
ing one another, give assurance." There are also "dovetailed revelations" for Saul
and for Ananias. Saul is blinded by a vision, and Ananias is directed "to a line of
action which will bring him to the knowledge of Saul's complementary vision." A
"main concern" of St. Luke "in the Annunciation story is to show with what objective certainty God has assured Mary (and through her, the Church) of her Son's
divine messiahship." Mary is "given the effect of the previous vision [to Zechariah]
as a confirmatory sign."[80]

Farrer likewise states that Mary herself appears as a "glorified figure" as the
woman clothed with the sun in Revelation 12. He admits that the application of
this passage to Mary has been "disputed," but "mistakenly, indeed." Farrer asks,
rhetorically, "How could St John write of a new Eve who bears the Messiah to crush

the old Serpent, without even thinking of Mary?" But the woman is "not primarily the figure of Mary nor, indeed of a *new* Eve." Rather, "it is the figure of Eve, that is, of woman, attaining the fulfilment of the promise implicit in the curse laid upon her in Eden." In Mary the ecclesia of God gives birth to the heavenly Man, becoming the mother of Christ. This "has all the dignity of a heavenly birth," Farrer states, "and the Mother becomes a heavenly figure." The image of Mary is thus fulfilled, so that she is "the embodiment of the Community in the physical bearing of *the* Child of God, the fruit of all Eve's travail."[81] And the fulfilment of all images.

6

Poetical Inspiration and Literary Interpretation

The paragraphs of the New Testament are "more like poetry" than the instructional pamphlet "thrown in with the sewing machine," Farrer explains, and "those who suppose that the problems of exegesis can be solved by writing dictionaries, theological or otherwise, are mistaken."[1] Definitions and instructions often fail to grasp poetical meaning. The "prophets and apostles alike are inspired by a quasi-poetical movement of images," and "the sort of criticism of most use for getting to the bottom of the New Testament is often more like the criticism we apply to poetry than we might like to expect."[2] Inspiration stands at a "midway point between poetry and metaphysics" and "actively communicates with both." In this way, the "subjective process of inspiration is essentially poetical, [and] the content it communicates is metaphysical."[3] Scripture's vital meanings may elude us if we neglect its poetical and literary interpretation.

Farrer's understanding of poetical inspiration and divine inspiration is based on his theological understanding of images. In *The Revelation of St. John the Divine,* for example, Farrer notes that the visions of the prophets of Israel "existed for St. John and his contemporaries in the form of written texts." John, in turn, "looked at the written records of these ancient visions until they fused into fresh shapes, expressive of a fuller truth." Again, this was a rebirthing of the images of Judaism, a "fusion and new-minting" of biblical images that, for John, "would naturally be a literary process."[4] Indeed it is best understood as a literary process with theological significance.

In *A Rebirth of Images,* Farrer explains that his method is "to introduce into the field of scriptural divinity a known method of poetical analysis."[5] The poetic imagination "gathers and unites its materials with a subtlety which no conscious contrivance could aspire to," which means that "we may spend years in putting asunder what an intuitive instant sufficed to join."[6] With these words, Farrer seems to make a dramatic departure from the conventional wisdoms of biblical criticism. He asks, rhetorically, "Do we see men most really when we let ourselves love them, and even poetize a bit about them, when we let our minds free to respond to them, or when we take them to pieces with analytical exactitude?"[7] Farrer commends an intuitive awareness of texts and meanings that goes beyond rational analysis and quasi-scientific methods of biblical study.

For Farrer, the study of images in Revelation and the study of "the process of inspiration by which they are born in the mind" are one study.[8] In this regard, "both Apocalypse and gospel are inspired writings; by a divinatory process the author shapes new images out of old words."[9] The biblical images of, say, St. Paul are not "unconnected in the Apostle's mind, they attract one another and tend to fuse, but they have their own way of doing this, according to their own imagery laws, and not according to the principles of conceptual system."[10] We must acknowledge the independence and integrity of the biblical images in themselves.

Divine inspiration is poetical. For example, "poetry, for the prophet, is a technique of divination, in the poetic process he gets his message," Farrer states. The prophets' minds were "charged with the word of God," and it is "obvious" that the "poetry itself was the method of divination."[11] The prophet and the poet share "the technique of inspiration," each moving "an incantation of images under control." Of course there are substantial differences between the poet and the prophet relative to the technique of inspiration, because the "controls are not the same, and therefore the whole nature and purpose of the two utterances go widely apart." In short, Farrer states, "the poet is a maker, the prophet is a mouth-piece."[12] The poet as maker may "say what the Muse prompts him to say."[13] But the prophet's own person is lost as the prophet speaks, "and the person whose utterance the words express becomes the person of the Lord." Otherwise the prophet "would never have dared to give his words as the words of a God who avenged falsification with death."[14]

With respect to the poet as "maker," Hefling observes in "Farrer's Scriptural Divinity" that *A Rebirth of Images* is subtitled *The Making of St. John's Apocalypse*. Hefling states that "no one knew better than Farrer" that "a 'maker' is by derivation a poet, just as a poem, in Greek, is a thing made, and by studying the 'making' of Revelation," Farrer was "studying the process that gave birth" to Revelation. So Farrer sought to understand "how the making was done, how the poem came into being in the mind of the poet," and he used "methods of investigation that had something in common with those of literary criticism." Farrer applied these literary methods to other New Testament books "in the conviction that they too, in their own way, are poetic works." Hefling notes that since the poetic making is "unpredictable" in its process and "unique" in product, the "workings" of the poet's mind can only be understood "by retracing the imaginative process of making through a sympathetic exercise of one's own imagination," thereby reconstructing the work of the New Testament writers by thinking their thoughts after them.[15] The scriptural texts may thus be approached in terms of the poetical and imaginative process that led to their creation.

Farrer chooses the abrupt ending of the Gospel of Mark (which he described as "one of the most famous and the most discussed of critical problems") to "illustrate the quasi-poetical character to be found in the New Testament writings." Mark 16:1–8 states that after the Sabbath, Mary Magdalene, Mary the mother of James, and Salome went to Jesus's tomb very early on the first day of the week to anoint his body. As they approached the tomb, they wondered who would be able to roll away the large stone for them, but at the tomb they found the stone had already been rolled back. There they encountered a young man dressed in a white robe, and he told them that Jesus "has been raised; he is not here." The young man also instructed the women to tell Jesus's disciples and Peter that they would see Jesus in Galilee. But the women fled from the tomb, "for terror and amazement had seized them, and they said nothing to anyone, for they were afraid." Farrer states that the remaining verses of Mark 16 "have no defensible claim to be genuine," and so the Gospel of Mark ends starkly "with the flight of the women from the empty sepulchre."[16]

With wry humor Farrer dismisses the possibility that Mark "ever wrote, or meant to write, any more," after speculating that perhaps the heavy hand of an official descended on his shoulder just as he reached the words "for they were afraid," and "the saint's literary career came to an abrupt conclusion," or that after Mark finished the book with a different ending, "his housekeeper used the last page of it to light the fire, and he always told his friends that he would rewrite it one day, but he never did." The fewer the better, says Farrer concerning these speculations, and he concludes that the text ends at Mark 16:8.[17]

With a much more serious tone, Farrer reiterates this conclusion in *St Matthew and St Mark*, stating that "it is immoral to invoke accident" relative to the ending of the Gospel of Mark, "whether physical accident, such as the damaging of the unique original before even St Matthew saw a copy; or personal accident, such as St Mark's death or arrest in the middle of a sentence, when he had a couple more paragraphs only to write." Accidents of this kind are possible, Farrer states, "but they are not at all likely."[18] He looks elsewhere to explain the ending.

Farrer acknowledges the difficulty of the ending of Mark's Gospel and considers it in literary terms. The story itself "contains hints of all sorts of future things which cannot in any case form part of its concluding narrative—the descent of the Spirit, the mission to the Gentiles, and the fall of Jerusalem." The objection that it "could not end so" means "the conclusion lacks poetical inevitability, just that." The "strong poetic expectations" built up in the Gospel of Mark are disappointed by the conclusion, "and we cannot believe that such a writer could have written so ill." Therefore, Farrer concludes, the debate over the ending "is a literary debate: and if we try to defend the abrupt ending, we must do it by literary arguments." Farrer's purpose is not to vindicate the merits of his argument about the ending of Mark's Gospel, but to persuade that "it is the proper sort of argument for the purpose, and that it belongs to the *genre* of literary criticism."[19] Farrer states toward the end of "Lecture VIII" in *The Glass of Vision* that "we have discussed the ending of St. Mark, not to prove a thesis, but to show what sort of argument is appropriate."[20] The ending provides a kind of case study to illustrate Farrer's literary method of biblical interpretation.

Farrer admits that the ending of the Gospel of Mark may not have "the ring of finality" in the "ear of the student of Attic oratory" or "the student of biblical Greek in general," but the story may be different "in the ear of the reader of St. Mark." Farrer notes that Mark "builds up his own rhythms, which gradually work themselves into our heads as we read his gospel through from the beginning."[21] In *A Study in St Mark,* Farrer again uses a musical metaphor to defend the ending of Mark's Gospel, stating that "the scene at the empty tomb is a final chord which draws together, echoes and concludes the preceding music."[22] He also states that Mark did not include an account of Christ's return because "he would not have felt that it brought the story to any sort of an end." There was no end for Mark "short of the end of the world," and he "could not carry the Gospel history on to the end of the world."[23]

And if in his day Farrer placed himself outside the mainstream of biblical interpretation, today he has a measure of support. Frank Kermode states in *The Genesis of Secrecy* that Farrer's reading of the ending of Mark's Gospel was "an outsider's interpretation" that was "condemned as it were by institutional intuition." But Kermode prefers Farrer's understanding "to interpretations that arise from the borrowed authority of the institutionalized corrector, and presuppose that the prime source of our knowledge of the founder of Christianity will necessarily be compliant with whatever, for the moment, are the institution's ideas of order."[24] In any case, Farrer would say, the ending of Mark's Gospel illustrates the appropriateness and use of his literary method for biblical interpretation.

The Method of Narrative Criticism

Farrer's method of study anticipates the approaches of "narrative criticism," which appeared more than thirty years later, its "discovery" at that time seeming to be something new. For example, David Rhoads writes in his preface to *Mark as Story: An Introduction to the Narrative of a Gospel,* that the project began when he asked his collaborator, Don Michie, "a friend from the Department of English, to show my students of New Testament Introduction how to read one of the gospels as one would read a short story." In the lecture that followed, Michie "talked about the suspense in the drama," "spoke of Jesus as a character struggling to get his message across," and "showed how the conflicts come to a climax in Jerusalem." Rhoads describes this lecture as an "initial eye-opening experience."[25]

The introduction to *Mark as Story* likewise states that "analyzing the narrative involves understanding not only the world of the story but also the impact which it may have on the reader." This method treats the text as a "unity" and serves "to reveal the narrative as whole cloth." Experiencing the narrative as an independent unity makes it possible for the reader to "participate in the world of the story."[26] Rhoads and Michie provide "an analysis of Mark's narrative along the lines of inquiry provided by contemporary literary criticism," including in their work chapters on rhetoric, settings, plot, and characters.[27]

Richard Edwards explains the method of narrative criticism in a more recent study. The "narrative critic," he explains, "tries to understand the *world of the narrative,* a unified entity which is the specific environment presented within the narrative," and "as each story progresses, more information becomes available and serves as the basis for the construction of that world."[28] He also states that "examining the *story* precisely and discovering how it influences the hypothetical implied reader will also help clarify where real readers, in specific cultural contexts, have overlooked, revised, or replaced certain elements of the story."[29] In narrative criticism, "characters are defined as individuals or groups presented/portrayed in the world of the narrative."[30]

Edwards applies this method to the Gospel of Matthew, noting that it is "a narrative of the life of Jesus. It is not an essay, a letter, or a theological treatise but a story which moves continually from a beginning to its conclusion."[31] Like Farrer, Edwards understands the biblical text in literary terms.

Edwards identifies eleven "disciple character-shaping incidents" in the Gospel of Matthew, including the "Call of Peter, Andrew, James, and John (Matt. 4:18–22)," the "Walking on the Water (Matt. 14:22–33)," and the "Disciples Meet the Risen Lord (Matt. 28:16–20)." In these narrative incidents, the implied ("text-connoted") reader receives information in the narrative that serves "*either* to add a new, distinct trait to the disciples *or* to modify one or more of the currently applicable traits."[32] In this regard, Farrer would say the reader gains a new appreciation of the disciples and Christian faith by character-shaping *images.*

A recent paper by Jeffrey Peterson describes Farrer as "a pioneer narrative critic" and "in some respects an interpreter half a century ahead of his time" in "the light cast on the Gospels by narrative criticism and related approaches." The "recognition of the Gospels as works of rhetorical art and the attempt to discern the literary patterns ordering their materials are now the rule rather than the exception," he adds.[33] In this light, Farrer's "unorthodoxy" is perhaps less startling than it once seemed, and the basics of his method may now be understood as a valuable application of narrative criticism.

The Interplay of Biblical Narratives

Farrer states that Mark's "poetical magic" appears in the gospel's "rhythmic repetition," so that "one paragraph subtly echoes another, emphasizing persistent themes and throwing variations into relief."[34] For purposes of comparison, Farrer identifies a sequence of events in the Gospel of Mark: a woman anoints Jesus at supper; Jesus gives his sacramental body to the disciples at supper; Jesus says to the disciples, "After I am risen again I will go before you into Galilee"; Jesus admonishes his disciples in the garden ("especially three of them") to watch; and the disciples flee, including a youth who lost his linen cloth to escape.[35] Farrer compares this section with the sequence in which Joseph obtains Jesus's body from Pilate; Jesus's body is wrapped in a linen cloth and buried; the three women bring perfumes to embalm the body; a youth in a white stole urges the women to tell the disciples that Jesus goes before them to Galilee, "as he had said to them (at the Supper)"; and "the women flee, saying nothing to anyone."[36]

Farrer identifies several common features in these two narrative sequences, including the perfuming of Jesus's body by a woman relative to the intended perfuming of Jesus's body by the three women; Jesus's prophecy that he will precede his disciples to Galilee relative to the explicit recalling of the prophecy by the youth; Jesus's giving of his sacramental body to the disciples relative to the attempt by disciples to "obtain and vainly wall up his physical body"; the "symbolical part" played by a loincloth (which is a "rare" word, not used elsewhere in Mark's Gospel); the presence of "'a lad' (again the word is confined to this pair of texts) 'clad in' some named garment"; and "a sudden catastrophe falls on disciples," prompting them to "react in the same way—by flight."[37] Farrer states that "the firm ending to the Gethsemane episode prepares us to find a firm ending in the last words of the sepulchre episode."[38]

Farrer also states that the three texts about the boy in the garden, the shrouding of Jesus by Joseph, and the boy in the tomb are held together by "verbal echoes" and the name of Joseph. Joseph the Arimathean begged Pilate's permission to bury Jesus, and Joseph the patriarch begged Pharaoh's permission to bury Israel. Farrer states that "a Jew could not hear the story of a Joseph who fulfils the pious duty of burial under difficulties, without thinking of Joseph the patriarch, so he could not hear of a boy who leaves his coat in his captors' hands and escapes without thinking of the same patriarch; the story of Joseph and Potiphar's wife being a favourite moral tale for the instruction of the young."[39]

Joseph the patriarch was stripped by his eleven false brothers, stripped by Potiphar's wife, "buried in prison," and believed by his eleven brothers to be dead. But he subsequently appeared to his brothers "as though alive from the grave, clothed in a robe of glory as the man of the king's right hand," and identified himself to them as Joseph. His brothers, however, "could not answer him, *for they were confounded.*" Similarly, the women at the tomb were "unable to speak, *for they were afraid.*" Farrer states that "a glance at the Greek Old Testament will show the exactness of the verbal parallel." Joseph overcame "the shame and terror of the eleven who had sold him, and St. Mark's readers will know that Jesus is going, in Galilee, to overcome the shame and fear of the eleven who had deserted him." The Gospel of Mark is a complete narrative. Thus Farrer's literary method leads to his conclusion concerning its ending: "The poem ends with finality at the words 'for they were afraid.'"[40] Farrer's method allows comparison and striking insights concerning narrative sequences in Mark's Gospel and other biblical texts—even if some of his comparisons seem far fetched.

Questions about the ending of Mark's Gospel are best answered when the text is approached as poetry. With respect to the ending, Farrer states that "the further we go into the question, the more clearly we see that St. Mark's words are shaped by a play of images and allusions of the subtle and elusive kind which belongs to imagination rather than to rational construction." Even if the ending of Mark's Gospel has "a clumsiness about it" and "is not good poetry," it is "still poetry, and our dissatisfaction with it (if we still feel dissatisfaction) is a poetical discontent."[41] If poetical texts are not understood as poetry, much will be lost in their interpretation.

Critical Controversy and Literary Interpretation

Farrer's understanding of poetical inspiration and literary interpretation proved, in his day, to be intriguing (and sometimes startling) in application. It was also controversial. David Jasper states that "there were two major critical attacks on *The Glass of Vision* in the 1950s," a theological attack by H. D. Lewis and a literary attack by Dame Helen Gardner.[42]

In *The Business of Criticism,* Gardner states that "it would not, I think, have been possible for a Christian before this generation to use such a phrase as the 'poetry of St. Mark.'" She states that Farrer "approaches the literary criticism of the New Testament with a mind steeped in secular literature both ancient and modern, and he shows himself fully aware of the parallels between what he is doing and what is being done by modern critics of poetry." The "abruptness" of the ending of Mark's Gospel, she asserts, "demands a literary solution" for Farrer, who has "whole-heartedly" adopted the methods of modern literary criticism. Gardner tracks Farrer's analysis of the ending of Mark's Gospel in terms of his literary method relative to theme, recurring phrases, narrative sequences, images with symbolic meaning, and the parallel sections of Mark's Gospel discussed above.[43]

Gardner continues her critique of Farrer by stating that when the Gospel of Mark is "considered as a work of literature," it "is seen as a great effort of symbolization, which we shall apprehend as we concentrate upon the lesser symbols which it integrates into its total pattern, until we see them all cohering into a structure of meaning." With this reading, she states, Mark "is seen to have no need to give us narratives of the Risen Lord's appearances to the disciples. His whole gospel is a great and complex symbol of the Resurrection, faith in which is its presupposition."[44] Gardner disagrees with this assessment and states that she is "dissatisfied because this method does nothing to illuminate, and indeed evaporates, St. Mark's sense of what we mean by historical reality, the 'Here and Now' of our daily experience, the 'Then and There' of memory, by which I do not mean detailed precision of testimony, but the deep sense of 'happening.'" She also finds it difficult to believe that "the first readers of St Mark would have been as ingenious in picking up references as is suggested."[45]

For Gardner, the attempt to proceed backward from a finished work to understand the way the writer's mind works is "like weaving ropes of sand." With respect to Farrer's use of the story of Joseph the patriarch and how it relates to the ending of Mark's Gospel, she states that if the name Joseph prompted an unconscious "reminiscence" for St. Mark, " it does not very much concern us." But "if it is intended to suggest that St. Mark was modeling his narrative consciously on the story of Joseph, the notion cannot, I think, stand examination." Gardner disagrees with Farrer's narrative parallels, and she argues that "the motives of the flight of Joseph and the young man's flight are entirely different: Joseph was saving his honour, the young man losing his, if that is what the loss of the white garment signifies." The "main point" of Joseph's self-revelation to his brothers was "their ashamed recognition of him." Gardner concludes that "conscious literary influence does not work like this," that literary criticism of this kind "leaves an impression of intellectual frivolity, as if the critic were concerned with anything and everything except what mattered to the writer and what matters to his readers."[46] In effect she states that Farrer does not provide an authentic literary criticism of the Gospel of Mark.

Gardner seems most concerned that Farrer's approach "is oblivious of, and often impatient with, the historical." Farrer, she insists, does not do justice to the historical reality of Christ. She states that Mark's Gospel is differentiated from other "messages of salvation" by "the assertion that something has happened in the world of history," and Farrer's literary method of interpreting scripture "does not explain a prime historic fact; that for centuries Christian emotion directed towards the historic person of Jesus Christ, true God and true Man, has found in the

Gospels the strength of its own conviction that 'Christ walked on this earth.'"[47] In a later book Gardner also objects that Farrer's critical methods made the author of Mark's Gospel "into a disembodied imagination."[48] For Gardner, Farrer's literary approach is disconnected from the historical and saving realities of the gospel.

H. D. Lewis provides another critique of Farrer's literary method of scriptural analysis. He points out that Farrer ascribes authority to "dominant Biblical images, or at least to the images that have the main place in a certain religious tradition." The problem is that Farrer "seems to me quite mistaken in ascribing this finality to the images as such, even when considered closely in relation to each other and their contexts." Lewis acknowledges that Farrer "has helped us to appreciate . . . the play of religious images and the fact that they seem to have a life of their own." But he warns that Farrer's emphasis on images can have unintended and unhelpful consequences. Lewis acknowledges that "new images, or the extension of old ones, evolved in the first place in the more spontaneous operation of imagination as such, or at least in detachment from express religious stimulation, may come to do excellent service for religion as the prompters and vehicles of insights which might not be otherwise forthcoming." But these images "may also be distracting and direct attention to extraneous matters, and they may even corrupt the religious imagination by diverting its energy to concerns not consistent with religious ends."[49]

H. D. Lewis also notes the "perils" of the "creative power which religion releases," and argues that disregard of these perils "has often brought the 'enthusiasm' of which religion stands in continuous need into ill repute." Therefore, Lewis states, "religious imagination needs to be controlled," both in its "early stages where art and religion are peculiarly integrated, but also at other times when enlivened imagination is apt to centre attention on whatever matters happen to be most suitable to its own operation, matters perhaps of subsidiary or incidental importance for religion, or, it may be, inferior or even degrading in themselves." Again Lewis states that "we cannot put ourselves wholly at the mercy of the life of images— that way madness lies."[50] He warns that encountering the unbridled life of images can disrupt both faith and sanity.

H. D. Lewis acknowledges that Farrer would say "that it is not *any* 'life of images' that he has in mind, but rather a particular life of images" that is subject to divine control. Lewis disagrees with this "supposition that the divine control is exercised primarily and directly on the religious images." For Lewis, "it seems highly artificial to suppose that God works primarily in the world through His 'given images' and not more directly in the very substance of living." In this regard, Lewis states that the imagination "is not a thing apart, but a feature of a total experience, and it has its material on which to work." The imagination "is not some odd separate gift of imagination that Shakespeare had, but imaginative insight into what life is like, and the more there is insight of this kind in the exercise of imagination, in distinction from the sheer precipitation of one image by another, the finer it is."[51]

Lewis warns that imagination should not be understood as a realm of existence separate from the rest of life. It "never works quite in a vacuum, and the rightful stress today on the importance of 'image thinking' will become one-sided unless we bear in mind also the need for imagination to be duly integrated with living." The "moral" of Lewis's theme "is that the images which figure in religious belief have their proper significance in relation to the experiences which they sum up and reflect and whose life they help to sustain." Images must "be anchored in experience and never allowed to take wing very far on their own." Lewis does acknowledge that "we must award a very prominent place to the work of imagination in giving sharp and impressive delineation of the course which religious experiences take, both in themselves and as a leaven of life as a whole, for the individual and his society," but it is necessary to remain "sensitive to the inherent dynamic of the image and sufficiently conversant in a general way with the facts out of which it arises to be informed by the images and not misled." In short, Lewis states, "we need to be imaginatively at home in the real world."[52] Gardner believes that Farrer neglects biblical history in his literary interpretations of scripture, and H. D. Lewis believes that Farrer neglects facts and the real world for the sake of images.

Farrer responded to both Gardner and H. D. Lewis with good-natured and characteristic self-deprecation concerning his "comparison between divine revelation and poetic 'inspiration'": "Miss Helen Gardner demolished the literary side of my comparison in her Riddell Lectures, and Professor H. D. Lewis the theological in *Our Experience of God*." However, Farrer was willing to consider "salvaging some elements of truth" from his "indiscretions."[53]

Farrer acknowledges that H. D. Lewis's "criticism is based on the very reasonable contention that revelation is fundamentally a personal encounter."[54] But, Farrer states, the analogy of revelation to poetry and the analogy of revelation to personal encounter "are not rivals to one another, nor do they lie in the same plane." In short, "it seems that God's encounter with us must be a sort of encounter, analogous to our encounters with men; and that the parables or symbols through which God teaches us to imagine his action must be some sort of symbols parallel, perhaps, to the symbols of valid poetry."[55] These analogies of revelation are neither contradictory nor inconsistent.

Farrer also upholds his method of literary interpretation by a return to the book of Revelation in "Inspiration: Poetical and Divine." He follows "the growth of images in St. John's mind from the beginning of his vision." Images abound in Farrer's five-page discussion of Revelation. For example, "Jesus is the Sun—anyhow, the Sun's day is the Lord's Day; and it is on this day that St John has his rapture and sees the Lord of Sunday, the Christ of the Resurrection; and he sees him with a countenance that shines like the sun at midday." Jesus "is the First and the Last in the great week of the world's ages; his is the Sunday of creation and, when the week of history has run through, his, in his Advent, is the Sunday of universal regeneration."[56]

After "St John has seen the countenance of Glory on earth, presented in the person of Jesus Christ," he is translated to heaven by his next vision "to see Glory enthroned in the person of the Father." In the right hand of the Almighty is "the book of his purpose, the book of prophecy, or of destiny," sealed with seven seals. Again Farrer draws out the unity of the biblical narrative in terms of transformed images: "As the seven seals are broken one by one, the destiny of the world will begin to unroll in seven successive acts: like the seven days of action by which God in the beginning both created the world, and appointed the Sabbath, and with it the sacred week imposed on Israelite observance, and transformed in Christian experience." No one is able to open the book until "the Lamb endowed with the sevenfold plenitude of spirit breaks one by one the seven seals of the book, and as he breaks them a series of seven events, a 'week' of divine judgements unrolls, the first of three such weeks, which taken together give shape to the Apocalypse and carry it forward to its destined consummation."[57] The Christ, the Lamb, is the Lord of the week, Lord of the Day of the Sun, and filled with the sevenfold full-ness of Spirit.

In terms of the literary parallels relative to the inspired writing of scripture, Farrer states that a poet "is trying to create a piece of verbal music in which sound and sense have each their part to play." One or another "will often take the lead and require to be checked by the others," but "the total set of formal requirements challenge a writer's invention to the harmonious satisfaction of them all together." An inspired writer such as St. John "is not set to create a pleasing or even a noble piece of verbal music." Rather, an inspired writer "is the mouthpiece of the Spirit in revealing mysteries."[58]

Farrer states that religious seers and secular poets may seek inspiration in simi-lar ways, but this "fact casts no light whatever on the fundamental mystery of divine inspiration." The English poet Percy Shelley "uses certain methods to set his imagination acting; and this gives his imagination scope to act. St John uses similar methods; and this gives the Holy Ghost scope to move his imagination." Images give the clairvoyant, or the poet, an opportunity to project images from within. John (like Shelley) "is also within himself, but so (in his belief, which we share) is the Spirit of God." The Creator "everywhere underlies the creature," but "at certain points he acts in, as, and through the creature's mind." Farrer states that imagination plays "a part" in this process. In "such an employment," imagination is "suppled and made responsive or creative," and "there will surely be an analogy here to the workings of the poetic mind." But the creative expression "in the two sorts of case will be widely different; and so will be the significance of the product."[59] For all his genial self-deprecation in response to Gardner's and Lewis's criticism, Farrer strongly upholds his position in terms of relating (and distinguishing) poetic and divine inspiration.

Farrer responds directly to Helen Gardner's criticisms in "On Looking below the Surface." Here he again begins his reply with good humor and humility, stating that "Miss Gardner would not have selected such a butterfly as me to break upon her wheel, but for the circumstance that I had happened to call attention to the parallel between the typological exegesis of Scripture and the sort of poetry-criticism which Mr Empson and in some places Charles Williams and other writers had endeavoured."[60] Farrer bows respectfully to his challenger.

Yet Farrer concedes nothing in terms of his literary method for interpreting scripture. He states that "analogies are not more than partial, and all parallels, if we allow ourselves to be misled by them, are misleading." He is willing to use helpful parables, and he is willing "to determine by sense and judgement" the merits of "poetical (and let us say Shakespearian) criticism" as a parable for exegesis of the Gospels. Various authors of literature have cultivated "double senses and willful ambiguities," and entire works have been "written or conceived on partially concealed symbolical patterns." For example, Farrer notes that "it is useless to stick to the plain moral or narrative sense and avert your eyes from piercing beneath the surface when you are travelling through a medieval masterpiece such as Dante's *Divine Comedy*."[61] Much of the meaning of such texts will be lost if the reader refuses to "look below the surface."

Farrer understands Gardner's judgment to be that "Shakespearian and so-forth critics who interpret by means of hidden patterns, undisclosed allusions, or willful ambiguities" have "overdone their part" and "largely exhausted their usefulness." But "in the biblical field, it is not clear that the method she criticizes has so limited a scope of proper use; and it is still less clear that the time has come when we ought to be calling a halt to its activities." Indeed, Farrer states dramatically, "when she tells us that the world of Bible scholarship is now all too prone to seek after types and to elaborate allusions, it makes me rub my eyes and wonder if I am awake."[62] Gardner's criticism needs a reality check.

Farrer admits that there are "alternative methods" beside typology for "tackling the unity and order of a synoptic Gospel," but historical biography, he insists, is not one of them. Furthermore, "to suggest that the typological approach is displacing the historical is misleading." Farrer in effect states that he is not such a "wild interpreter" as to deny "the whole historical content of St Mark's Gospel," to declare "every line in it to be a tissue of typological allusion," or to "deny that St Mark, when he had a plain unvarnished tale to tell, could tell it, anyhow to the extent of a single episode or anecdote."[63] In this regard, Gardner also seems to overlook Farrer's correlative understanding of inspired image and historical event, as presented in "Lecture III" of *The Glass of Vision*.[64] Farrer notes that Gardner admits the presence of "explicit typological references" in the New Testament but argues against "implicit typological allusion" by the same New Testament authors. The "authors who are in places openly allusive or symbolical are those likely to be disguisedly so elsewhere; as we see in Dante or in Spenser," he observes.[65]

In response to Gardner's position that "explorations of undisclosed symbolism or patterns seldom help her to understand the meaning of an author," and that "what pays is the careful examination of the thing he directly says," Farrer offers the "Adamic interpretation" of Romans 7. In Romans 7:9–10, Paul writes, "I was once alive apart from the law, but when the commandment came, sin revived and I died, and the very commandment that promised life proved to be death to me." In an essay on typology, Farrer states that in Romans 7, Paul "meditates on himself as a typical redeemed sinner, by applying to himself the history of Adam, a man alive without the law once, but then the law (thou shalt not eat of it) was given him, and he incurred death (by eating)."[66]

Although the name "Adam" does not appear in Romans 7, Paul is passionate in describing "his own predicament" in terms of an undisclosed symbol. Yet he says in Roman 5, in essence, that "the Adam-predicament is (or was) his predicament." Farrer asks, "Does it cast no light on what he is saying about himself, to realize that it is an applying of the type of Adam, and not a free psychological or moral analysis?" Paul's "undisclosed Adamic typology in Romans 7 is made possible by the background offered in the explicit Adam typology of Romans 5."[67] If we neglect the typological connection between Romans 5 and Romans 7, our understanding of Romans 7 will be seriously limited. Farrer defends his poetical and literary method of exegesis in light of Gardner's criticisms, and he is convincing. Even if some of Farrer's particular applications may be questioned, he defends his *method* (with characteristic humility): "Bad practice should not discredit an art."[68] Farrer concedes nothing to Gardner.

7

Divine Action and Human Freedom

Farrer's understanding of the interplay of divine and human action is carefully balanced and nuanced to present both the pervading reality of divine initiative and the human freedom that allows true choice, responsibility, and subjectivity. In acknowledging a divine will, he states, "we are confronted with the supreme theological paradox—two wills on different levels, the creative and the creaturely, shaping our human existence."[1] Regarding Farrer's understanding of this paradox, Edward Hugh Henderson states that the act of free human obedience to God is "something the person freely does, and it is at the same time something God does."[2] Farrer clearly recognizes the interplay of human free will and divine initiative as one of the most important and challenging of theological questions. The human being "is the image of God in so far as he both has a will and wills the supreme good according to his ability."[3]

This central paradox of faith touches every aspect of the Christian life, including prayer: "Unless our prayer is God's act of will it lacks the distinctive grace of prayer; unless it is an act of our will it has not the merit of being our prayer at all, but breathed through us without becoming ours."[4] True prayer calls for the action of divine and human will together.

The dynamics of the divine-human interplay are complex. One finite excludes another in the sense that "I am enacting my life, you are enacting yours: I cannot enact yours nor you mine." But, Farrer states, "every mystery of religion," and indeed "the very possibility of any spiritual religion," presupposes that the finite does not exclude the infinite. The activity of God's will in us does not displace our free will. In fact, God's activity in us is necessary for us to exercise our will as free agents. We do not act in isolation from God, who created us and upholds our existence. By the grace of God we can choose and act, but we still must do our own choosing and acting. Farrer states that "in some true sense the creature and the Creator are both enacting the creature's life, though in different ways and at different depths: in the second cause the first cause operates."[5] In this way "the action of a man can be the action of God in him" and "our religious existence is an experimenting with this relation."[6]

The divine-human interplay cannot be analyzed in an exact way. Farrer explains that "when we try to appreciate the experience of men receiving (as they deem) divine communication, we find ourselves time and again in doubt where to put the point of punctuation between the divine and the human."[7] However, divine initiative and primacy characterize any divine-human relation. It is "the conviction of orthodox religion" that God's "activity is primary, and ours very secondary, in any interchange."[8] Farrer terms this interplay of divine and human "double personal agency," or simply double agency. And "upon this double personal agency in our one activity turns the verbally insoluble riddle of grace and freewill, or of Godhead and Manhood in Christ's One Person, or of the efficacy of human prayer; indeed there is no issue theologians discuss which is not conditioned by it."[9] Accordingly, Henderson notes that "the idea that God is a personal agent who acts in the world by double agency" is the "most important and pervasive of Farrer's philosophical ideas."[10]

Farrer's understanding presupposes the otherness of God and God's will. Farrer upholds the "positive and practical value in asserting the otherness of God," which means that "we exercise our relation with him as a personal relation." God's "life is personal to him, it is not ours." God "has a will after which we enquire, a judgment to which we submit, a forgiveness we implore, a succour we seek." Therefore, Farrer states, "the personal character of our relation" with God "is the very form of it" and "not a metaphorical trapping" that can be dismissed.[11] In this divine-human relationship we encounter the otherness of God's will.

Farrer states that "both the divine and the human actions remain real and therefore free in the union between them."[12] It is God's will "to set his creatures free, and only to act for them by acting in them."[13] Our free agency is not displaced by God's action: "Our wills are ours to make them God's, and it cannot be done by proxy."[14] God's grace "does not remove our own initiative." Rather, the one who receives divine grace experiences that "the more it's God, the more it's I: and the more it's I, the more it's God."[15] Martin Luther likewise states that God "creates and preserves us without our help; but he does not work in us without us, because it is for this he has created and preserved us, that he might work in us and we might cooperate with him."[16]

In terms of this mutual divine-human activity, Farrer asserts that "our neighbour is a piece of the divine handiwork, still in the making; it is the process of creation still continuing, which demands our instrumental cooperation." It is the theist's belief that God "is making our neighbour. And yet our neighbour is, in some measure at least, making himself." It is possible in the creating of a single life to accommodate two wills, "one all-knowing and divine, the other fallible and human." The finite does not exclude the infinite. However, it "would be a blasphemous equalization" to describe these as "two wills side by side." Instead, they are "as it were, ranged in depth, the one behind the other, the one acting through and in the other."[17] Farrer states that "it may be a tolerable language to describe our action as a cooperation with God; but such cooperation is nothing like cooperation with our fellow-beings, when our work and their work dovetail together in specifiable ways."[18] Even when we cooperate with the divine will, God transcends us as the infinite exceeds the finite.

As a practical matter, "divine will is understood as purpose, recognised in its effect, and embraced by consent." But "invisibility" covers the "'causal joint' between infinite and finite act," and "the traditional problems of Grace and Freewill are simply expressions" of that invisibility.[19] We cannot be too exact about the actual interplay of divine grace and human freedom. We must, in effect, be reverently agnostic about the "causal joint" of divine and human act. We cannot identify the precise timing, extent, or manner of divine activity in any human act, since we do not know "the modality of the divine action we cannot pose the problem of their mutual relation."[20]

This open-endedness concerning the specifics of the divine-human relation has pastoral implications as well. Farrer states that a spiritual guide need only contradict "any proposition which denies the personal reality of either the human action or the divine, or which, admitting both, inverts the hierarchy and makes the divine action consequent upon the human rather than *vice versa*."[21] In this way, Farrer also draws out a pastoral application from a rather delicately balanced question of philosophical theology.

Human freedom must not be overborne or there would be no humanity. If God were to divinize any creature in a way that removed "its distinct creaturely nature," this "would be exactly equivalent to its annihilation."[22] But it is possible in humanity in general—as in Christ—for the supernatural to enhance and intensify without removing human nature.[23] Grace can work to perfect or complete human nature without destroying it. The "act of condescension by which God serves his creatures in making them make themselves," Farrer explains, "is no self-annihilation on God's part, it is simply the appropriate use of his power; it is the only way to make such a world as this is."[24]

Farrer states that "grace is an action of the Creator in the creature." When God "acts in the rational creature he is pleased to act in that creature's mental and voluntary life, bringing them into his own."[25] This delicate paradox may also be seen from the human side. Henderson states concerning Farrer's double agency that "we experience the action of God in our own experience of active faith, and we experience it as an action that takes effect without forcing us against the grain of our nature as free agents."[26] Our finite humanity is not displaced by divine action. Farrer states that our "free and sovereign" actions of thought and decision "are the chief occasions and, as it were, organs for the reception of actual grace." And this opens the paradox: "Our most free acts are those most purely and pellucidly expressive of a will sovereign over all."[27] We are most fully ourselves when our lives most fully reflect God's will.

The divine and human share an "I-Thou" relation of free but greatly unequal subjects. The divine-human relationship is personal and reciprocal. The human subject does not stand as an "it," an impersonal thing, before God, and God does not stand as an "it" before the human person.[28] God can be revealed and known as subject through the experience of human freedom and subjectivity. And Farrer (characteristically) presents this understanding in terms of various images.

Farrer states in *A Science of God?* that "the thinking creature," the human person, "reveals God in two different ways. He serves as a sketch and he serves as a pencil." The person "serves as a sketch by simply being personally what he is—a thinker, a chooser, a maker, and a lover." It is "on the model of these characteristics or activities that we form whatever conception of deity we ever do form."[29] Human freedom and capacity can reveal the divine in an analogous way. As Thomas Aquinas states, we may know God through sense experience and "as He is represented in the perfections of creatures."[30]

The person also reveals God as a pencil "by putting into the hand of God an instrument with which God can directly express his purpose, his character and his thought." But acting as "a pencil in God's hand is not given to a man in virtue of his mere humanity. No doubt the possibility is in some sense always there, but to realise the actuality is another matter."[31] The human will must consent. Farrer states that people "are called upon to make a once-for-all decision, since they are capable of it."[32] They may reveal the divine by choosing to live the divine will.

In *A Science of God?* Farrer explains that "the Creator of the world is not to be compared with those bad novelists who make up the plot of their story first, and force the characters to carry it out, all against the grain of their natures." God does not overbear our free will, even in the name of our salvation. God "is like the good novelist who has the wit to get a satisfying story out of the natural behavior of the characters he conceives." This is done by God "identifying himself" with the characters, "and living them from within."[33] God may work in us and through us, but without displacing our own agency.

In a similar way, Dorothy L. Sayers, a mystery writer and playwright, states that if a literary character "becomes *merely* a mouthpiece of the author, he ceases to be a character, and is no longer a living creation." And "if *all* the characters speak with their author's voice, the whole work loses its reality, and with it, its power."[34] Real characters are not clones of the creator of their story or play, and they may act in ways other than the author would have chosen in his or her own life. According to Sayers, the "free will of a genuinely created character has a certain reality, which the writer will defy at his peril."[35] Of course, there would be no literary character without the maker, and there would be no creature without the creator, but both character and creature are to be respected by the creator in the integrity of their agency.

Sayers states that the human maker desires to create a self-conscious being and can not, but he or she finds "approximate satisfactions for this desire in procreation, in such relations as those of a playwright with his actors, and in the creation of imaginary characters." In all these relations, the human maker "is conscious of the same paradoxical need—namely, the complete independence of the creature, combined with its willing co-operation in his purpose in conformity with the law of its nature." This "insistent need" reveals "the image of the perfect relation of Creator and creature, and the perfect reconciliation of divine predestination with free created will."[36] Sayers provides a literary vision of double agency at its best.

In the sermon "The Potter's Clay," Farrer uses Jeremiah's image of a working potter to describe the interaction of God's initiative and human will in the saving process. This process begins with divine initiative, but it requires human cooperation. Farrer explains that "nothing comes of the clay—or our life, that is—but what God makes of it. The clay makes no shapes for itself except crazy shapes by distortion of the shape intended; a crack here, a lump there, a ruin and a confusion." The clay is a mess without the maker, but "the true life of the clay is to spin into symmetry under the maker's hand." Our true completion is the fulfillment of who and what God would have us to be, and God will guide us to completion, as the potter shapes and completes the pot. But this is not a passive or inevitable process for us. Our free will is never removed or overwhelmed—"nothing results . . . by the mere force of the hand unless the clay is fit and responds." God does not force us into the shape of salvation. Farrer notes that "the clay in which God works is our free will, and though he gave it us, it is free."[37] A divine-human cooperation is necessary for our completion in the saving process. Farrer's doctrine of double agency underlies the sermon's pastoral application of the image of the potter's clay.

The saving relation of the divine and the human is ongoing. There is "no escaping" from God's hands, Farrer states, "there is never a moment for the clay, when the potter is not doing something with it," and "his fingers are on us all the time." God will not fumble with the clay, although he will meet faults in us—"a lump here, and there it crumbles; here something too stubborn and resistant, there nothing firm enough to make a shape." Through it all, the process of God's interaction with us for salvation is ongoing, as the potter's work with the unformed clay is creative and ongoing.[38]

Farrer allows for different outcomes as this process unfolds. If we love God's will, "we take the shape of it. If we are lazy and selfish, his fingers oppose us and make war on us, and crumble us back into obedience." But when we repent, "without a moment's delay the ever-active fingers are moulding us back into the divine image." Farrer states that "the skill of the divine potter is an infinite patience of improvisation," so that "no sooner has one work gone awry than his fingers are pressing it into the form of another."[39] God continues to reach out to us to shape our lives for salvation, and we continue to choose whether to accept God's invitation.

For Farrer, the "entry of the divine into the human may be called inspiration on the one side, and co-operation on the other."[40] In this regard, the effects of the Holy Spirit may be seen as we freely accept and cooperate with the divine activity in our lives. The Spirit does not overpower us or manipulate us, not even for salvation. We can accept or resist the divine grace that saves us. Our free will is the "instrument" of the Spirit, Farrer explains, and the Spirit does not force us. Instead, the activity of the Spirit "is like the rising water of the tide, ready to fill every cranny that opens in the reef it engulfs, yet forcing no openings that are not offered."[41] Grace completes but does not destroy or diminish nature. The Spirit will fill us and guide us, but not against our wills, so that the Spirit is "constantly active to insert his inspirations wherever we do not frustrate him by our selfishness and inattention."[42] Human unwillingness or incapacity is always the limiting factor in the divine-human interaction.

A Union of Wills

God relates to humanity "as the will which underlies our existence, gives rise to our action and directs our aim."[43] But we are free to choose, to accept or reject the divine initiative. God's will "takes actual effect in what his creatures do of their own motion."[44] Faith competes with many other attitudes in the human heart, but "as we allow our faith to act, it obtains mastery."[45]

Our faith in God is necessary for union with God. Farrer offers the story from Matthew's Gospel of Jesus's temptation by Satan to participate in "an arranged experiment on the divine will." The temptation was for Jesus "to jump from the temple cornice and see what the God of the temple would do." But, Farrer states, "since it was not the divine will that he should jump, his jumping would not be an experiment on the divine will," and "arranged experiments on the divine will are ruled out."[46] And so Jesus answers the devil, "'Do not put the Lord your God to the test.'"[47] Farrer notes in *A Science of God?* that "we cannot reason ourselves into faith by the experiment of union with God's will; for the experiment is no experiment unless it is an act of faith." It is impossible to "perform the spiritual act of uniting our wills with the will of a God in whom we do not yet believe."[48]

With respect to prayer, Farrer states in *Faith and Speculation* that the "main intention" of a believer's prayer is "union of will, and this the divine action deepens, if the man will accept it." From this union of divine and human will, "and from it alone, the blessings of sanctity spring." These "manifold" blessings include "the sheer fact of harmony with our Creator," as well as "participation in his acts, purposes and affections, so far as it concerns us to enter into them."[49]

Mutual participation of the divine and human for salvation is a central theme in Anglican theology. For example, John Booty states that Richard Hooker's use of the term "participation" provides a key to Hooker's meaning in book 5 of *Of the Laws of Ecclesiastical Polity* in terms of "the mutual participation of deity and humanity in Christ enabling that mutual participation of Christ in us and we in Christ, which constitutes Christ's body, the church."[50] The shared participation of Christ and faithful Christians means that "by vertue of this mysticall conjunction wee are of him and in him even as though our verie flesh and bones should be made continuate with his."[51]

Human Action and Divine Will

The only way for human beings to "have experimental knowledge of the will behind our will" is "by opening our will to it, or sinking our will in it; there is no other conceivable way." This sinking of the human will in the divine will, Farrer explains, may be done "by an obedient attention" to God's will.[52] Prayer "is a sincere seeking of the divine will."[53] Devotion to God's will means that "we can place ourselves in his action as we suppose it to be disclosed."[54] Farrer states that "it is through our freewill that we know the divine will, which is the divine being."[55] And "if we recognise a creative will within and behind our own, we acknowledge it as that by which we are what we are, as though it were the wellspring out of which we draw our being."[56] We may know the divine will as we engage it in our actions.

Farrer states that "we cannot touch God except by willing the will of God. Then his will takes effect in ours and we know it."[57] W. Mark Richardson explains Farrer's position: "We know God by willing God's will, intending to align ourselves with divine purposes as we recognize them in finite effects."[58] Henderson likewise states that "if we are to know God and God's way of acting in the world, we must first act in a way that will allow us to know God; that is, we must act in a way appropriate to the reality we seek to know."[59]

But, Farrer urges, it "is no small matter" really to think and heartily embrace the will of God.[60] There is no "apparatus," no "set moves" or "technique of method" for relationship with God. It simply concerns "a relation of will to will," and this "can be achieved at any time, by thinking, deciding, acting."[61] Indeed, Farrer states, "will, action, the creative moment in man, is the only object of consideration which opens a dimension of metaphysical depth, or promises to let through a single ray of uncreated light."[62] Of course, through the entire process it is God who is "uniting us with his will; and when we say 'with his will' we are saying 'with himself.'"[63]

According to Farrer, we enter into the divine action "simply by acting, whether the action be a movement of thought or an employment of the hand."[64] By embracing the divine will it is possible to "experience the active relation of a created energy to the Creator's action."[65] We may know God's will in the specific contexts of our lives. Indeed the "only one divine will we can touch" is "what God wills us to do here and now; and we can only find it by embracing it."[66] This is "the only possible way" to "experience the active relation of a created energy to the Creator's action."[67] We may know God's will by living out double agency.

To embrace God's will, Farrer observes, "is the same thing as to make a practical application, or use, of our relationship with God," so that the divine will acts as "the master, the guide and the inspiration of ours."[68] With respect to God's action sustaining or inspiring human action, Farrer states that "the divine assistance is experienced simply in its effect." And this involves double agency, which Farrer illustrates with an image: "To be assisted by a mountaineer I must put my weight on a rope; to receive the divine assistance I have only to think or act my trust in God."[69] We may know God's will as we act in faith, so that God's will is known in our action.

The will of God is not "a shy secret hidden somewhere under the root of our mind, and there to be dived for."[70] The divine will is not remote from humanity in a distant or otherworldly way. God's will "is chiefly displayed in the demands of our environment" and "written across the face of the world."[71] It is, in fact, "a particular will for every man in every situation." Because of the particularity of God's will for each person and situation, there are no repeatable "experiments" concerning the divine will.[72] It is no more possible to concoct experiments for the divine will than to "look for a note of music through a microscope."[73] God's will for us is not a fixed object like a rock that is inert and unmoving through many circumstances. But God's will may be incarnated and it is to be known dynamically in the specific contexts of each person's life.

God's will is predictable in its tendency to draw us into concern and service for others. God's will is "projected on our practical environment," and it is "my neighbour's good."[74] This means that the divine will is discerned relationally and interpersonally. To see God's will, "I must look at my neighbour," so that "if Dives wants to find the will of God, let him look at Lazarus. How much longer are his sores to go untended or his hunger unfed?"[75] We may know God's will as we help others.

Stated poetically, embracing God's will comes from the *heart* of the faithful person. It is "a personal act," and "all a man's personal acts spring from his heart." Personal acts are "no mere automatic performances." The believer "means them; and certainly it is from his heart, and not anyone else's, that they must come." But embracing the divine will is not "locked" inside the human heart. The divine will may be known and lived in terms of the full range of human action. Farrer states that "a man can speak to his friends from the heart, and from the heart do them services. The acts by which the will of God is embraced similarly employ the hands and the tongue."[76] Our "most contemplative adoration rests upon a practical relation of our action to the divine."[77] Our most contemplative adoration involves double agency.

Jesus embraced the will of God by his *actions* in the world: "by stopping the brawl at his arrest and by surrendering himself; . . . by maintaining his royal claim before the High Priest and the Roman Governor; by refusing the doped wine, by praying for his executioners, and by all his acts and words on that memorable day."[78] It is likewise through actions in the world that God's will may be embraced by people today. Farrer states that "the embracing of God's will has the whole of a man's conduct for its outward expression" and that "there is nothing of importance he does which cannot in principle express his obedience."[79] We may incarnate God's will in our lives.

Farrer affirms the paradox of divine transcendence and immanence. God is "remote by what he is," but God "is familiar in what he does, for he identifies his thought with the thing he makes and moulds his care for it on its existence." God "is not far from any one of us, for by him we live and move and have our being."[80] In a similar way, William Porcher DuBose states that "all our relation to Jesus Christ is of that immediate, direct, and intimate character which is possible for us only with God Himself." We live and move and have our being "only by and in God Himself," only through Christ's "own immediate presence and action in us."[81] These statements epitomize DuBose's theology of the process of salvation, by which it is possible to share Christ's life and move toward actual completion of the saving process in our lives.[82]

We live in relationship with God "not only as souls or persons," Farrer explains, "but as animals and even as parcels of physical stuff." God's will "is in the drawing of our breath and in the pulses of our heart; how much more in the movement of our affection or the aspiration of our hope!" God upholds our life, and we may engage the divine will in the exercise of our own will. "Above all," Farrer states, God "takes the form of our action when he inspires us, when we let our will be the instrument of his." It is not necessary to "scale heaven or strip the veil from ultimate mystery" for union with the divine. We may find and be found by God in this world, in the contexts of our life. God "descends into his creature and acts humanly in mankind," and God "has made it our calling that we should have fellowship with himself."[83] This involves living an incarnational spirituality, know-ing the extraordinary of God in the ordinary events of life, so that the divine will is embraced and known on a daily basis.

Farrer's understanding of double agency is close to that of Martin Luther King Jr., when King considers the disciples' failure to cast out a demon because of their lack of faith (Matthew 17:14–21). In the sermon "The Answer to a Perplexing Question," King notes Jesus's reminder that "they had been attempting to do by themselves what could be done only when their lives were open receptacles, as it were, into which God's strength could be freely poured." In short, their human agency alone was insufficient for the task. But faith makes double agency possi-ble. Although King does not use the term "double agency," he provides an appli-cation of it in terms of the American struggle for civil rights. Specifically he urges, "Racial justice, a genuine possibility in our nation and in the world, will come nei-ther by our frail and often misguided efforts nor by God imposing his will on way-ward men, but when enough people open their lives to God and allow him to pour his triumphant, divine energy into their souls."[84] He also states with respect to social evils that "moral victory will come as God fills man and man opens his life by faith to God, even as the gulf opens to the overflowing waters of the river." Or, in Farrer's terminology, double agency engaged will lead to the victory of racial justice.

Farrer's understanding of double agency has been appreciated by his commen-tators. Jerry H. Gill states that Farrer "has made a convincing case" that "our knowl-edge of God results from interaction with divine agency in the context of our individual lives."[85] Brian Hebblethwaite likewise states that the "hidden hand of God is perceptible" to us "in so far as we can detect a pattern embodying God's purpose for us, and experience in our own lives what it means to co-operate with his grace."[86] Both Gill and Hebblethwaite recognize Farrer's point that we may know and incarnate the divine will in the context of our own lives.

With respect to conversion, Farrer states in "Grace and the Human Will" that "no one becomes a Christian without antecedent conditions and present influ-ences" in terms of divine grace, and "no one becomes a Christian, but of his own will."[87] God forces no one into conversion, but we may accept God's promptings for conversion with our human will. Conversion involves double agency. In a sim-ilar way, DuBose states that "God redeems or completes no person except in and through the act of his own self-redemption or completion." Conversion is rela-tional, involving both the divine and the human. We cannot "redeem ourselves without God, nor can God without us—in an act which must be ours as well as His; it is a matter of God in *us,* which can mean nothing else than what *we* are and do and become through Him in us."[88] Conversion is as much an expression of God's life in us as it is an expression of our life in God.

Relational Knowing and Divine Will

Farrer points directly to a relational knowing of the divine will. As "humanity is only made amiable to us by being objectified in another face, so the expression (though not perhaps the influx) of grace is scarcely perceptible in ourselves—even where we do not distort and hinder it beyond recognition—but may be visible in others." Whether or not we are "on a level" with others in whom grace may be visible, "others are uniquely the instruments of grace towards us by being Christians before us, and talking us into the speech of faith, as those who reared us talked us into our mother tongue."[89] We may recognize God's activity in others and know God through others. As Farrer notes in the sermon "A Share in the Family," "We all lay like idiots in the cradle; and idiots we should have remained, if no one had smiled us into smiling back, or talked us into talking."[90] We learn our humanity through others. As Robert M. Cooper states, "We only begin truly to discover ourselves in otherness, in the other," so that the human "finds himself only in finding and in being found by the other, and it is not really until that point that finally there is human being at all."[91] We may know God and ourselves in contexts of relationship.

Farrer's relational understanding of what it means to be a human being and how we may know divine grace is close to that of Scottish philosopher John Macmurray, who states that "it is only in relation to others that we exist as persons" and that our knowledge of each other and ourselves is realized only through mutual self-revelation "when we love one another." This is "the basic fact of our human condition."[92] We do not live as human beings in isolation. Personal knowledge requires personal relationship with the other.[93] As Macmurray states, we "live and move and have our being not in ourselves but in one another; and what rights or powers or freedom we possess are ours by the grace and favour of our fellows."[94] Our human lives are interconnected, and this interconnectedness provides a basis for our knowing. Human life "is indeed a common life, and we depend upon one another at every point in a thousand ways."[95]

Scottish theologian John Macquarrie, an Anglican, expresses a similar view of what it means to be a person, noting that an "individual is only a person in so far as he or she stands in relation to other individuals" and that "the autonomous isolated I is something less than a person."[96] Macquarrie uses the phrase "There is no I without a thou,"[97] which parallels Macmurray's statement that the "I" constitutes both the "I" and the "You" in the phrase "You and I."[98] Macquarrie acknowledges that persons constitute a community, "but equally these persons are formed by the community."[99] He notes that "the human person is, from the beginning, a relational being, bound up with other persons in what is sometimes called a web of life."[100] Macquarrie and Macmurray, like Farrer, assert that human beings are relational beings who become themselves and understand their world in the context of relationship with others. And our human relationships provide the context and paradigm for knowing God, whom we know relationally.

The Paradox of Obedience and Freedom

For Farrer, the mystery of grace is "seen in the influx of the divine will into the human. And if this is where the true mystery lies, then it cannot be that the recognition of grace can undermine an appreciation of man's free will." The "chief occasions" and "organs for the reception of actual grace" are "free and sovereign actions on our part, anyhow actions of thought and of decision." Humanity would be enslaved if we were "told that our destiny is determined not by our free acts, but by conditions or influences outside our control."[101] Our freedom to choose, therefore, is at the heart of our capacity to love and share in relationship. Indeed, our freedom to choose is at the heart of our capacity to receive grace.

Henderson, remarking on Farrer's double agency, states that "cooperating with God's action, we are more ourselves and more free than when we act without regard to God."[102] We are not liberated or empowered by acts of will that isolate us from God and others, although these acts may provide a temporary illusion of power or control. Paradoxically we are most free and complete as human beings when we incarnate the divine will in double agency. For example, with respect to prayer, Farrer states that "no act of will we ever make is so centrally and vividly our own as this act which God performs in us." This double agency "is what we really intend and really desire, this is when we are really ourselves." In this double agency of prayer, it is God "who originally created us free" who also "is renewing our creation and our freedom."[103] Our prayer may then embody the divine-human will.

Farrer understands the paradox of divine and human interaction in relational terms: the "grace active in the human will so operates as to make us dependent upon one another, as well for the supernatural gifts of God, as for natural charities and blessings."[104] We need God, we need the church, and we need one another. We discover our freedom as we let it go. We know God's will as we live it. We find ourselves as we give ourselves in the love of God.

Notes

Preface

1. Daphne Mack, "'Greatest Anglican Mind of 20th Century' Is Conference Focus," *Episcopal News Service,* October 26, 2004, http://www.episcopalchurch.org/3577_53360_ENG_HTM.htm (accessed June 10, 2006). Farrer has also been described by the bishop of Oxford as "the one genius produced by the Church of England" in the twentieth century. Richard Harries, "'We Know on Our Knees . . . ": Intellectual, Imaginative and Spiritual Unity in the Theology of Austin Farrer," in *Divine Action: Studies Inspired by the Philosophical Theology of Austin Farrer,* ed. Brian Hebblethwaite and Edward Henderson (Edinburgh: T. & T. Clark, 1990), 30.

2. M. P. Wilson, "St John, the Trinity, and the Language of the Spirit," *Scottish Journal of Theology* 41 (December 1988): 471.

3. Charles C. Conti, "Editor's Preface," in *Reflective Faith: Essays in Philosophical Theology,* by Austin Farrer (London: SPCK, 1972; Grand Rapids, Mich.: William B. Eerdmans, 1974), viii.

4. Farrer's first theological writings were published in 1933. See Austin Farrer, "A Return to New Testament Christological Categories," *Theology* 26 (June 1933): 304–18; and Austin Farrer, "Review of *The Life of Jesus* by Maurice Goguel," *Theology* 27 (October 1933): 229–30.

5. There are several bibliographies of Farrer's publications. See "Bibliography of Writings about Austin Farrer and Other Research Aids," in *Captured by the Crucified: The Practical Theology of Austin Farrer,* ed. David Hein and Edward Hugh Henderson, 197–208 (New York and London: T. & T. Clark, 2004); Charles Conti, "A Chronological List of Austin M. Farrer's Published Writings, 1933–1981," in *For God and Clarity: New Essays in Honor of Austin Farrer,* ed. Jeffrey C. Eaton and Ann Loades, 191–200 (Allison Park, Pa.: Pickwick Publications, 1983); Charles C. Conti, "Chronological List of Published Writings: 1933–1973," in Farrer, *Reflective Faith,* 227–34; "Chronological List of Published Writings by Austin Farrer 1933–76," in *A Hawk among Sparrows: A Biography of Austin Farrer,* by Philip Curtis, 250–57 (London: SPCK, 1985); and "An Annotated Selection of the Works of Austin Farrer," in *Jacob's*

Ladder: Theology and Spirituality in the Thought of Austin Farrer, by Charles C. Hefling Jr., 127–32 (Cambridge, Mass.: Cowley Publications, 1979).

6. Brian Hebblethwaite, "Austin Farrer's Concept of Divine Providence," *Theology* 73 (December 1970): 542.

7. Susan Howatch, introduction to *Saving Belief: A Discussion of Essentials,* by Austin Farrer (London: Mowbray and Morehouse, 1994), viii.

8. Charles Conti, preface to *Words for Life,* by Austin Farrer, ed. Charles Conti and Leslie Houlden (London: SPCK: 1993), viii.

9. Philip Curtis, "The Rational Theology of Doctor Farrer," *Theology* 73 (June 1970): 249. Curtis states that he "once tried to summarize the 300 pages of *Finite and Infinite* and found I had 120 pages of notes." See Austin Farrer, *Finite and Infinite: A Philosophical Essay,* 2nd ed. (1943; reprint, Westminster: Dacre Press, 1959).

10. Curtis, "The Rational Theology of Doctor Farrer," 256.

11. Basil Mitchell, interview by the author, Woodstock, England, August 16, 2006.

12. Curtis, "The Rational Theology of Doctor Farrer," 249.

13. Margarita Stocker, "God in Theory: Milton, Literature and Theodicy," *Journal of Literature & Theology* 1 (March 1987): 71.

14. Chad Walsh to Katharine Farrer, March 18, 1969, Letters from Various Friends I folder, box 4, Farrer Papers, on deposit in the Modern Papers and John Johnson Reading Room, Department of Special Collections and Western Manuscripts, New Bodleian Library, University of Oxford (hereafter cited as Farrer Papers). Used with the kind permission of the Trustees of the K. D. Farrer Trust.

15. Martin W. Jarrett-Kerr, CR, to Katharine Farrer, December 31, 1968, Notable Persons folder, box 4, Farrer Papers. Used with the kind permission of the Trustees of the K. D. Farrer Trust.

16. John H. Heidt to Katharine Farrer, December 31, 1968, Letters from Various Friends II folder, box 4, Farrer Papers. Used with the kind permission of the Trustees of the K. D. Farrer Trust.

17. Katharine Farrer to Austin Farrer, February 26, [probably 1935], set 4, box 2, Farrer Papers. Used with the kind permission of the Trustees of the K. D. Farrer Trust.

18. Katharine Farrer to Austin Farrer, March [probably 1935], set 5, box 2, Farrer Papers. Used with the kind permission of the Trustees of the K. D. Farrer Trust.

19. Conti, "Editor's Preface," in Farrer, *Reflective Faith,* viii–ix.

20. I. M. Crombie, "Farrer, Austin Marsden (1904–1968)," in *The Dictionary of National Biography, 1961–1970,* ed. E. T. Williams and C. S. Nicholls (Oxford: Oxford University Press, 1981), 350.

21. Austin Farrer, preface to *The Glass of Vision* (Westminster: Dacre Press, 1948), ix. The book consists of Farrer's eight Bampton Lectures for 1948.

22. Austin Farrer, "Whereinsoever Any Is Bold, I Am [Sexagesima]," in *Bible Sermons: A Course Preached in the Chapel of Pusey House, Oxford,* by Christopher Evans and Austin Farrer (London: A. R. Mowbray, 1963), 37.

1. Farrer's Background, Method, and Perspective

1. Crombie, "Farrer, Austin Marsden (1904–1968)," 349.

2. A. N. Wilson, *C. S. Lewis: A Biography* (London: Collins; New York: Norton, 1991), 245n. Wilson likens Farrer to C. S. Lewis, who was never promoted to professor at the University of Oxford. Lewis died on November 22, 1963. After Lewis' death, Farrer stated in a letter that "it was an odd experience having to eulogize him in Magdalene Chapel in the presence of colleagues who had lived with him and made nothing of him." Austin Farrer to Martyn Skinner, December 10, 1963, Letters from Austin Farrer and Katharine Farrer to Martyn Skinner folder, box 4, Farrer Papers. Used with the kind permission of the Trustees of the K. D. Farrer Trust.

3. Curtis, *A Hawk among Sparrows*, 103–5.

4. Walter Hooper, e-mail message to the author, April 13, 2005.

5. Curtis, *A Hawk among Sparrows*, 143–44. Caroline was sent to a Rudolph Steiner school in Kent.

6. Ibid., 144–45. Katharine's detective novels (the Inspector Ringwood trilogy) were *The Missing Link* (London: Collins, 1952), *The Cretan Counterfeit* (London: Collins, 1954) (a Crime Club Choice), and *Gownsman's Gallows* (London: Hodder and Stoughton, 1957). Paperback first American editions of this trilogy were reprinted by Rue Morgue Press of Boulder, Colorado. *The Missing Link* and *The Cretan Counterfeit* were reprinted in 2004, and *Gownsman's Gallows* was reprinted in 2005. Katharine's "off-beat novel" was *At Odds with Morning* (London: Hodder & Stoughton, 1960). She also translated Gabriel Marcel's *Être et Avoir*. See Gabriel Marcel, *Being and Having,* trans. Katharine Farrer (Westminster: Dacre Press, 1949). Curtis states that Marcel's *Être et Avoir* was "the work from which Farrer drew the distinction between mysteries and problems which he used in the Bampton Lectures." Curtis, *A Hawk among Sparrows*, 145. See Farrer, "Lecture V," in Farrer, *The Glass of Vision*, especially 79–82, for Farrer's "distinction between mysteries and puzzles."

7. Susan Howatch, *Absolute Truths* (New York: Alfred A. Knopf, 1995), 562 (author's note). Farrer's understanding of suffering is discussed in chapter 4, "The Problem of Evil."

8. Curtis, *A Hawk among Sparrows*, 145.

9. Ibid., 168.

10. Howatch, *Absolute Truths*, 562 (author's note).

11. Curtis, *A Hawk among Sparrows*, 168–69.

12. Francis Douglas Price, "Speech at Keble London Dinner" (January 7, 1969), 2. Unpublished manuscript available in the Keble College Archive. Used by the kind permission of the Warden and Fellows of Keble College, Oxford. Price was subwarden at Keble College.

13. Price, "Speech at Keble London Dinner," 2. A warden is approximately equivalent to a dean in an American college.

14. Walter Hooper, *C. S. Lewis: A Companion & Guide* (London and San Francisco: Fount and HarperSanFrancisco, 1997), 655. An entry on Farrer appears in a "Who's Who" section of this book by Hooper on Lewis.

15. Price, "Speech at Keble London Dinner," 2.

16. Hooper, *C. S. Lewis*, 655.

17. Price, "Speech at Keble London Dinner," 2–3. See 2 Kings 9. Jehu, newly anointed king over Israel, mounted his chariot and went to Jezreel. As he approached Jezreel, the sentinel said, "It looks like the driving of Jehu son of Nimshi; for he drives like a maniac" (2 Kings 9:20).

18. Howatch draws from Farrer's *Love Almighty and Ills Unlimited, Said or Sung,* and *A Celebration of Faith* to introduce chapters in *Absolute Truths.*

19. Howatch, *Absolute Truths,* 27. See Austin Farrer, "The Potter's Clay," in *Said or Sung: An Arrangement of Homily and Verse,* by Austin Farrer (London: Faith Press, 1960), 82; also in Austin Farrer, *Austin Farrer, the Essential Sermons,* ed. Leslie Houlden (London SPCK; Cambridge, Mass.: Cowley, 1991), 18 (subsequent page citations for *Essential Sermons* are in parentheses following page citations for the original sources). Preached in Trinity College Chapel, Oxford. See Jeremiah 18:1–11. The character Charles Ashworth narrates *Absolute Truths* and makes this statement concerning the potter and the clay. His spiritual director, Jon Darrow, states that "a sermon a day by Austin Farrer will do you far more good than the latest volume from some learned German theologian." Howatch, *Absolute Truths,* 411.

20. Howatch, *Absolute Truths,* 562 (author's note).

21. C. S. Lewis, preface to *A Faith of Our Own,* by Austin Farrer (Cleveland: World Publishing, 1960), 8.

22. Hooper, *C. S. Lewis,* 654.

23. Susan Howatch, introduction to Farrer, *Saving Belief,* viii (Howatch edition). *Saving Belief* presents the texts of lectures by Farrer to undergraduates. It was first published in 1964 by Hodder & Stoughton in London, and in 1965 by Morehouse-Barlow in New York. The 1994 Howatch edition, unfortunately, changed the original pagination.

24. John Hick, foreword to Farrer, *Reflective Faith,* xv.

25. E. L. Mascall, "*In Memoriam,* Dr. Austin Farrer," *Church Times* (London), January 3, 1969, 15.

26. Crombie, "Farrer, Austin Marsden (1904–1968)," 350.

27. Charles Hefling, "Farrer's Scriptural Divinity," in Hein and Henderson, *Captured by the Crucified,* 150. An example of Farrer's unorthodox biblical interpretation is seen in his willingness to "dispense" with the widely accepted hypothesis that the common non-Marcan gospel writings of Matthew and Luke are derived from a common source ("Q"). Farrer states that the Q hypothesis "wholly depends on the incredibility of St. Luke's having read St. Matthew's book," and "that incredibility depends in turn on the supposition that St. Luke was essentially an adapter and compiler." When two documents "derive from the same literary region" and contain "much common

material, some of it verbally identical," the "first supposition is not that both draw upon a lost document for which there is no independent evidence." Indeed, Farrer states, "St. Luke's own preface informs us that he writes 'in view of the fact that several authors have tried their hands at composing an account of the things fulfilled among us.'" If the possibility that "St. Luke had read St. Matthew (or *vice versa*)" is demonstrated, Farrer states, the Q hypothesis "falls by its own weight." Farrer upholds that possibility, offering a detailed analysis of Matthew and Luke and other biblical material. Austin Farrer, "On Dispensing with Q," in *Studies in the Gospels: Essays in Memory of R. H. Lightfoot,* ed. D. E. Nineham (Oxford: Basil Blackwell, 1957), 55–56, 62, 85. See Luke 1:1. E. L. Mascall states in a memoir on Farrer that "On Dispensing with Q" was a "challenging (and to some circles scandalous) essay." E. L. Mascall, "*In Memoriam,* Dr. Austin Farrer," 15.

28. C. K. Barrett, "Review of *St Matthew and St Mark* by Austin Farrer," *Journal of Theological Studies,* n.s., 7 (1956): 110. See Austin Farrer, *St Matthew and St Mark,* 2nd ed. (London: Dacre Press, 1966). This book "arose" out of the Edward Cadbury Lectures of 1953–54 (viii).

29. Hefling, *Jacob's Ladder,* xii.

30. Richard Harries, "Celebration of the Centenary of the Birth of Austin Farrer, October 11th, 2004," *Diocese of Oxford,* September 23, 2004, http://www.oxford .anglican.org/. Sermon preached by the bishop of Oxford at Oriel College, Oxford, on September 8, 2004.

31. Conti, "Editor's Preface," in Farrer, *Reflective Faith,* vii.

32. Hooper, *C. S. Lewis,* 654–55.

33. Austin Farrer, "Analogy," in *Twentieth Century Encyclopedia of Religious Knowledge: An Extension of The New Schaff-Herzog Encyclopedia of Religious Knowledge,* ed. Lefferts Augustine Loetscher (Grand Rapids, Mich.: Baker Book House, 1955), 1:38. This essay also appears as "Theology and Analogy 1, the Concept of Analogy," in Farrer, *Reflective Faith,* 64–68.

34. Austin Farrer, "Faith and Evidence," in *Saving Belief: A Discussion of Essentials,* by Austin Farrer (London: Hodder and Stoughton, 1964; New York: Morehouse-Barlow, 1965), 27 (17 in Howatch edition).

35. Farrer, *Finite and Infinite,* 27.

36. Dorothy M. Emmet, *The Nature of Metaphysical Thinking* (London: Macmillan, 1949), 105. Emmet's reference to "the infinite and the finite" may have been a passing acknowledgment of Farrer. She cites Farrer's *Finite and Infinite* on three occasions in *The Nature of Metaphysical Thinking.* See 39n1 and 186nn1, 2. Emmet was professor of philosophy at the University of Manchester.

37. Austin Farrer, *The Freedom of the Will* (New York: Charles Scribner's Sons, 1958), 49. An enlargement of Farrer's Gifford Lectures delivered at the University of Edinburgh, 1957.

38. Curtis, *A Hawk among Sparrows,* 49. Curtis was asked by the trustees of the Farrer estate to write a biography of Farrer (vii).

39. Farrer, "Lecture V," in Farrer, *The Glass of Vision*, 93–94. Farrer was the Bampton lecturer for 1948, and his eight Bampton Lectures were published as *The Glass of Vision*.

40. Austin Farrer, "The Christian Doctrine of Man," in *The Christian Understanding of Man*, ed. T. E. Jessop et al., The Church, Community, and State series, vol. 2 (London: George Allen & Unwin, 1938), 188; reprinted in Austin Farrer, *Interpretation and Belief*, ed. Charles C. Conti (London: SPCK, 1976), 74 (subsequent page citations for materials reprinted in *Interpretation and Belief* are in parentheses following page citations for the original sources).

41. Farrer, "Lecture V," in Farrer, *The Glass of Vision*, 86.

42. Ibid., 86–87.

43. Ibid., 90.

44. Austin Farrer, "Inspiration: Poetical and Divine," in Farrer, *Interpretation and Belief*, 41.

45. Ibid., 45.

46. Austin Farrer, *The Revelation of St. John the Divine: Commentary on the English Text* (Oxford: Clarendon Press, 1964), 24.

47. Austin Farrer, "Thinking the Trinity," in *A Celebration of Faith: Communications, Mostly to Students*, by Austin Farrer, ed. Leslie Houlden (London: Hodder and Stoughton, 1970), 75 (also Farrer, *Essential Sermons*, 79). Preached in Trinity College Chapel, Oxford, on Trinity Sunday, 1961.

48. Farrer, "The Magnet of God," in Farrer, *A Celebration of Faith*, 90. Preached in Christ Church Cathedral, Oxford, 1967.

49. Austin Farrer, "The Death of Death," in *The End of Man*, by Austin Farrer, ed. Charles C. Conti (London: SPCK, 1973), 9 (also Farrer, *Essential Sermons*, 58). Preached in Keble College Chapel, Oxford, 1968.

50. Farrer, "Gates to the City," in Farrer, *A Celebration of Faith*, 97.

51. Austin Farrer, "Mary, Scripture, and Tradition," in *The Blessed Virgin Mary: Essays by Anglican Writers*, ed. E. L. Mascall and H. S. Box (London: Darton, Longman & Todd, 1963), 50 (also Farrer, *Interpretation and Belief*, 123).

52. Austin Farrer, "Revelation and History," in *Faith and Speculation: An Essay in Philosophical Theology Containing the Deems Lectures Delivered at New York University in 1964*, by Austin Farrer (New York: New York University Press; London: Adam & Charles Black, 1967), 97.

53. Farrer, "Faith and Reason," in Farrer, *Reflective Faith*, 51.

54. Farrer, "Lecture V," in Farrer, *The Glass of Vision*, 90.

55. Farrer, "Nature and Creation," in Farrer, *Faith and Speculation*, 68.

56. Farrer, "The Empirical Demand," in Farrer, *Faith and Speculation*, 28.

57. Farrer, "The Rational Grounds for Belief in God," in Farrer, *Reflective Faith*, 7.

58. Farrer, "Faith and Reason," in Farrer, *Reflective Faith*, 56.

59. William Porcher DuBose, "Christian Defense," in *Unity in the Faith*, ed. W. Norman Pittenger (Greenwich, Conn.: Seabury Press, 1957), 242. This essay originally

appeared as "Christian Defense, or Apologetics," in *The Sunday School Teacher's Manual*, ed. William M. Groton, 2nd ed., pt. 3 (Philadelphia: George W. Jacobs, 1911), 76. See Robert Boak Slocum, *The Theology of William Porcher DuBose: Life, Movement, and Being* (Columbia: University of South Carolina Press, 2000), 15.

60. Farrer, "The Empirical Demand," in Farrer, *Faith and Speculation*, 35.

61. Ibid., 32.

62. Farrer, "Spiritual Science," in Farrer, *Faith and Speculation*, 36.

63. Farrer, "The Empirical Demand," in Farrer, *Faith and Speculation*, 28.

64. Farrer, "Mary, Scripture, and Tradition," in Mascall and Box, *The Blessed Virgin Mary*, 28 (also Farrer, *Interpretation and Belief*, 102).

65. Farrer, "The Prior Actuality of God," in Farrer, *Reflective Faith*, 189–90. This lecture was presented at Louisiana State University, Baton Rouge, and at Southern Methodist University in the autumn of 1966.

66. Farrer, "The Burning-Glass," in Farrer, *Said or Sung*, 108 (also Farrer, *Essential Sermons*, 20). Preached in St. Mary the Virgin, Oxford.

67. Ibid., 109 (also Farrer, *Essential Sermons*, 21).

68. Farrer, "Self-Reliance," in Farrer, *A Faith of Our Own*, 62–63.

69. Farrer, "Finding God," in *The Brink of Mystery*, by Austin Farrer, ed. Charles C. Conti (London: SPCK, 1976), 143. Preached in Trinity College Chapel, Oxford, 1956. See John 3:1–21.

70. Austin Farrer, "Epiphany," in *The Crown of the Year: Weekly Paragraphs for the Holy Sacrament*, by Austin Farrer (Westminster: Dacre Press, 1952), 13. See Matthew 2:1–12 and Mark 14:3–9.

71. Farrer, "Grace and Resurrection," in Farrer, *A Celebration of Faith*, 149 (also Farrer, *Essential Sermons*, 139). Preached in Mercers' Chapel, London, Lent 1963.

72. Farrer, "Creed and History," in Farrer, *Saving Belief*, 83 (69 in Howatch edition).

73. Farrer, "A Christian's Dilemmas, (1) Submission to God or Mastery of Nature," in Farrer, *A Celebration of Faith*, 125 (also Farrer, *Essential Sermons*, 127). Preached in Keble College Chapel, Oxford, 1966.

74. Farrer, "A Christian's Dilemmas, (2) Piety or Happiness," in Farrer, *A Celebration of Faith*, 130 (also Farrer, *Essential Sermons*, 131). Preached in Keble College Chapel, Oxford, 1966.

75. Farrer, "Heaven and Hell," in Farrer, *Saving Belief*, 146 (126 in Howatch edition).

76. Farrer, "The Potter's Clay," in Farrer, *Said or Sung*, 82 (also Farrer, *Essential Sermons*, 18).

77. Farrer, "Sin and Redemption," in Farrer, *Saving Belief*, 95 (79 in Howatch edition).

78. Farrer, "A Christian's Dilemmas, (2) Piety or Happiness," in Farrer, *A Celebration of Faith*, 130 (also Farrer, *Essential Sermons*, 131).

79. Farrer, "For a Marriage," in Farrer, *A Celebration of Faith*, 137. Preached at the wedding of David and Valerie Morris, September 10, 1966, at St. John's, Westminster.

80. Farrer, "A Christian's Dilemmas, (2) Piety or Happiness," in Farrer, *A Celebration of Faith,* 128 (also Farrer, *Essential Sermons,* 130).

81. Farrer, "Lent," in Farrer, *The Crown of the Year,* 22.

82. Austin Farrer, *The Triple Victory: Christ's Temptations according to Saint Matthew* (London and New York: Faith Press and Morehouse-Barlow, 1965), 91. *The Triple Victory* was the archbishop of Canterbury's Lent book.

83. William Porcher DuBose, *Turning Points in My Life* (New York: Longmans, Green, 1912), 87. See Slocum, *The Theology of William Porcher DuBose,* 8.

84. Farrer, "Trinity xxii," in Farrer, *The Crown of the Year,* 59.

85. Farrer, "Double Thinking," in Farrer, *A Celebration of Faith,* 28 (also Farrer, *Essential Sermons,* 87).

86. Saint Augustine, *Confessions,* trans. Henry Chadwick (Oxford: Oxford University Press, 1991), 148.

87. Farrer, "Double Thinking," in Farrer, *A Celebration of Faith,* 28 (also Farrer, *Essential Sermons,* 87).

88. Farrer, "Strength through Weakness," in Farrer, *A Faith of Our Own,* 42.

89. Farrer, "Walking Sacraments," in Farrer, *A Celebration of Faith,* 111. Preached at Edward Ryan's first Mass, in Holy Trinity, Northwood, on the evening of December 22, 1968.

90. Farrer, "Strength through Weakness," in Farrer, *A Faith of Our Own,* 42.

91. Farrer, "A Grasp of the Hand," in Farrer, *Said or Sung,* 37 (also Farrer, *Essential Sermons,* 210). Preached in Christ Church Cathedral, Oxford, on Christmas Day.

92. Farrer, "Strength through Weakness," in Farrer, *A Faith of Our Own,* 45; Farrer, "A Grasp of the Hand," in Farrer, *Said or Sung,* 37 (also Farrer, *Essential Sermons,* 210–11). "A Grasp of the Hand" is essentially the same sermon as "Strength through Weakness," though the former includes a concluding paragraph not found in the latter. This additional paragraph begins, "As to what the eternal Judge will say to those on his left hand, this is not the time to think; for to-day is a day of gladness, a day to ring all the bells in earth and heaven, because the love of God is born into the world, so strongly armed with weakness that it must prevail. Love is nowhere more truly omnipotent than in the manger; in the speechless child we adore the Word who made the worlds, the Son of the everlasting God, the express image of uncreated glory." Farrer, "A Grasp of the Hand," in Farrer, *Said or Sung,* 38 (also Farrer, *Essential Sermons,* 211).

93. Farrer, "A Grasp of the Hand," in Farrer, *Said or Sung,* 37 (also Farrer, *Essential Sermons,* 210). Farrer's appreciation for Jesus's "deputies of weakness" also includes Jesus's statement that by feeding the hungry, giving drink to the thirsty, welcoming the stranger, clothing the naked, caring for the sick, and visiting those in prison, we serve Christ. Farrer, "A Grasp of the Hand," 37–38 (also Farrer, *Essential Sermons,* 211).

94. Farrer, "The Commander's Love," in Farrer, *A Celebration of Faith,* 174 (also Farrer, *Essential Sermons,* 152).

95. Farrer, "Atoning Death," in Farrer, *Said or Sung,* 70 (also Farrer, *Essential Sermons,* 48). Preached in Trinity College Chapel, Oxford.

96. Farrer, "Walking Sacraments," in Farrer, *A Celebration of Faith*, 111.

97. Farrer, *The Triple Victory*, 63.

98. Farrer, "Reaping Faith," in Farrer, *The End of Man*, 56. Preached at Bletchingdon Harvest Festival, 1962. Also preached at St. Mary's, Primrose Hill, London, 1963.

99. Austin Farrer, "An Ordination Sermon," *Theology* 94 (May/June 1991): 166–67. Preached at the ordination of Rev. Richard Nevius, May 1961.

100. Farrer, "S. Mark," in Farrer, *Said or Sung*, 99 (also Farrer, *Essential Sermons*, 68). Preached in Trinity College Chapel, Oxford.

101. Farrer, "Committed Christians," in Farrer, *Said or Sung*, 147 (also Farrer, *Essential Sermons*, 183). Preached in Pusey House Chapel, Oxford.

102. As St. Paul says, "All have sinned and fall short of the glory of God" (Rom. 3:23).

103. Farrer, "S. Mark," in Farrer, *Said or Sung*, 99 (also Farrer, *Essential Sermons*, 68).

104. Alan Jones, "The Crack in the Heart," in *A New Conversation: Essays on the Future of Theology and the Episcopal Church*, ed. Robert Boak Slocum (New York: Church Publishing, 1999), 109.

105. " Farrer, "Idols," in Farrer, *The Brink of Mystery*, 90. Preached in Keble College Chapel, Oxford, on the Second Sunday after Epiphany, 1965.

106. Farrer, "The Charms of Unbelief," in Farrer, *A Faith of Our Own*, 15–16.

107. Austin Farrer, *Lord I Believe: Suggestions for Turning the Creed into Prayer*, 2nd ed. (London: SPCK, 1962), 9–10.

108. Farrer, "Sabbath and Sunday," in Farrer, *A Faith of Our Own*, 86.

109. Farrer, "Holy Otherness," in Farrer, *The Brink of Mystery*, 4–5 (also Farrer, *Essential Sermons*, 96).

110. Farrer, "Fish Out of Water," in Farrer, *A Faith of Our Own*, 140 (in Farrer, *Said or Sung*, 122).

111. Farrer, "You Want to Pray?" in Farrer, *A Celebration of Faith*, 143 (also Farrer, *Essential Sermons*, 106–7).

112. Farrer, "Ivory Towers," in Farrer, *A Celebration of Faith*, 200. Preached in Keble College Chapel, St. Luke's Day, 1965.

113. Farrer, "Soul-Making," in Farrer, *A Celebration of Faith*, 160 (also Farrer, *Essential Sermons*, 156). Preached in Little St. Mary's, Cambridge, on Whitsunday.

114. Farrer, "Considerateness," in Farrer, *A Faith of Our Own*, 199. Farrer draws on the hymn text by Charlotte Elliott: "Just as I am, without one plea, but that thy blood was shed for me, and that thou bidd'st me come to Thee, O Lamb of God, I come, I come." See Charlotte Elliott, "Just as I Am, without One Plea," in *The Hymnal 1982* (New York: Church Hymnal Corporation, 1982), 693.

115. Matthew 6:12.

116. Farrer, "The Burning-Glass," in Farrer, *Said or Sung*, 110 (also Farrer, *Essential Sermons*, 21).

117. Farrer, "Epstein's Lazarus," in Farrer, *The End of Man*, 29. Preached in New College Chapel, Oxford.

118. Farrer, "History and the Gospel," in Farrer, *A Celebration of Faith,* 45. This was the Hulsean Sermon, preached in Great St. Mary's, Cambridge, 1948.

119. Farrer, "You Want to Pray?" in Farrer, *A Celebration of Faith,* 142 (also Farrer, *Essential Sermons,* 105).

120. Farrer, "Human and Divine Habitations," in Farrer, *The End of Man,* 167. Preached in St. Barnabas, Oxford, at the feast of dedication.

121. Farrer, "Finding God," in Farrer, *The Brink of Mystery,* 140.

2. Farrer's Systematic Themes

1. Farrer, "How Can We Be Sure of God?" in Farrer, *A Celebration of Faith,* 61 (also Farrer, *Essential Sermons,* 172). Preached in the Cowley Fathers' Church, Oxford, 1967.

2. Farrer, "What Is Faith in God?" in Farrer, *A Celebration of Faith,* 71. Preached in St. Mary's, Oxford, 1960.

3. Farrer, "You Want to Pray?" in Farrer, *A Celebration of Faith,* 142 (also Farrer, *Essential Sermons,* 106).

4. Farrer, *Finite and Infinite,* x.

5. Farrer, "Grace and Resurrection," in Farrer, *A Celebration of Faith,* 147 (also Farrer, *Essential Sermons,* 137).

6. Farrer, "God's Will and Mine," in Farrer, *Words for Life,* 23.

7. Ibid., 23.

8. Farrer, *The Freedom of the Will,* 250.

9. Farrer, "A Share in the Family," in Farrer, *A Celebration of Faith,* 104 (also Farrer, *Essential Sermons,* 174). Preached for All Saints' Day.

10. Farrer, "Justifiable Analogy," in Farrer, *Faith and Speculation,* 126.

11. Farrer, "The Believer's Reasons," in Farrer, *Faith and Speculation,* 6.

12. Farrer, "Justifiable Analogy," in Farrer, *Faith and Speculation,* 126.

13. Farrer, "True Child of Man," in Farrer, *A Celebration of Faith,* 92. After Nebuchadnezzar boasted, "'Is this not magnificent Babylon, which I have built as a royal capital by my mighty power and for my glorious majesty?'" a voice from heaven declared to him, "'The kingdom has departed from you! You shall be driven away from human society, and your dwelling shall be with the animals of the field. You shall be made to eat grass like oxen, and seven times shall pass over you, until you have learned that the Most High has sovereignty over the kingdom of mortals and gives it to whom he will.'" This sentence was immediately fulfilled against Nebuchadnezzar. See Daniel 4:30–33.

14. Farrer, "True Child of Man," in Farrer, *A Celebration of Faith,* 92–93.

15. With respect to christology, it is interesting to note Farrer's understanding that "Jesus was the Christ, he was not a Christologist." He states that "the first century was the time for Christ to be Christ, and to achieve our salvation," but "not the time for Christ, or his work, to be rationally understood." Such understanding "was the work of after ages." Farrer, *The Triple Victory,* 57.

16. Farrer, "Creed and History," in Farrer, *Saving Belief,* 74 (60 in Howatch edition).

17. Austin Farrer, "The Theology of Morals," *Theology* 38 (May 1939): 333 (also Farrer, *Interpretation and Belief,* 177).

18. Farrer, "Very God and Very Man," in Farrer, *Interpretation and Belief,* 135.

19. Farrer, "Grace and Resurrection," in Farrer, *A Celebration of Faith,* 147–48 (also Farrer, *Essential Sermons,* 138).

20. Farrer, "Four Bible Sermons, (3) Lent 1," in Farrer, *The Brink of Mystery,* 31. Preached in Pusey House Chapel, Oxford, 1963.

21. Farrer, *The Triple Victory,* 44.

22. Farrer, "The Hidden God," in Farrer, *Words for Life,* 8.

23. Farrer, "The Magnet of God," in Farrer, *A Celebration of Faith,* 89. Preached in Christ Church Cathedral, Oxford, 1967.

24. Farrer, "A Share of the Family," in Farrer, *A Celebration of Faith,* 104–5 (also Farrer, *Essential Sermons,* 174).

25. Farrer, "The Magnet of God," in Farrer, *A Celebration of Faith,* 89.

26. Ibid., 89–90.

27. Farrer, *The Triple Victory,* 59.

28. Ibid., 60.

29. Ibid., 85.

30. Ibid., 32.

31. Farrer, "Grace and Resurrection," in Farrer, *A Celebration of Faith,* 148 (also Farrer, *Essential Sermons,* 138).

32. Austin Farrer, "Messianic Prophecy and Preparation for Christ," in *The Communication of the Gospel in New Testament Times, Some Recent Studies by Austin Farrer, C. F. Evans, J. A. Emerton, F. W. Beare, R. A. Markus, F. W. Dillistone,* SPCK Theological Collections 2 (London: SPCK, 1961), 6. This sermon was preached before the University of Oxford in 1958.

33. Austin Farrer, "The Everyday Use of the Bible," in *The Bible and the Christian: A Course of Sermons on the Bible Preached in the Chapel of Pusey House, Oxford* (London: A. R. Mowbray, 1957), 59–60.

34. Farrer, *The Triple Victory,* 54.

35. Ibid., 60.

36. Farrer, "The Christian Doctrine of Man," in Jessop et al., *The Christian Understanding of Man,* 190 (also Farrer, *Interpretation and Belief,* 76).

37. Ibid., 199 (also Farrer, *Interpretation and Belief,* 83).

38. Farrer, *Lord I Believe,* 59.

39. See Robert Boak Slocum, "Romantic Religion and the Witness of James DeKoven," in *To Hear Celestial Harmonies: Essays on the Witness of James DeKoven and the DeKoven Center,* ed. Robert Boak Slocum and Travis Talmadge Du Priest (Cincinnati: Forward Movement, 2002), 28.

40. Farrer, *The Triple Victory,* 60.

41. Austin Farrer, "Eucharist and Church in the New Testament," in *The Parish Communion: A Book of Essays,* ed. A. G. Hebert (London: Society for Promoting Christian Knowledge; New York: Macmillan, 1937), 82. Farrer makes this statement on the authority of "the doctrine of Colossians" and cites Colossians 1:15–20.

42. Farrer, "Providence, Mystery, and Evil," in Farrer, *The Brink of Mystery,* 7. Preached in Keble College Chapel, Oxford, 1965.

43. Farrer, *The Triple Victory,* 24.

44. Farrer, "Physical Faith," in Farrer, *The End of Man,* 15. Preached at St. Thomas's, Regent Street, London, on that saint's day.

45. Farrer, "Grace and Resurrection," in Farrer, *A Celebration of Faith,* 149–50.

46. Farrer, "A Share of the Family," in Farrer, *A Celebration of Faith,* 105.

47. Ibid., 105.

48. Farrer, "Lent iv," in Farrer, *The Crown of the Year,* 25.

49. Farrer, "A Grasp of the Hand," in Farrer, *Said or Sung,* 36 (also Farrer, *Essential Sermons,* 210).

50. Farrer, "Dying to Live," in Farrer, *Said or Sung,* 158 (also Farrer, *Essential Sermons,* 123). Preached in Trinity College Chapel, Oxford.

51. Farrer, "The Charms of Unbelief," in Farrer, *A Faith of Our Own,* 16.

52. Farrer, "The Burning-Glass," in Farrer, *Said or Sung,* 110 (also Farrer, *Essential Sermons,* 21).

53. Farrer, "The Charms of Unbelief," in Farrer, *A Faith of Our Own,* 18.

54. Farrer, "Humbug," in Farrer, *Said or Sung,* 46–51.

55. Farrer, "The Charms of Unbelief," in Farrer, *A Faith of Our Own,* 16–18.

56. Farrer, "Dying to Live," in Farrer, *Said or Sung,* 157 (also Farrer, *Essential Sermons,* 122).

57. Farrer, "A Grasp of the Hand," in Farrer, *Said or Sung,* 36 (also Farrer, *Essential Sermons,* 210).

58. Farrer, "Supporting Hands," in Farrer, *The End of Man,* 60. Preached in Queen's College Chapel, Oxford.

59. Austin Farrer, "Griefs and Consolations," in *Love Almighty and Ills Unlimited: An Essay on Providence and Evil, Containing the Nathaniel Taylor Lectures for 1961,* by Austin Farrer (Garden City, N.Y.: Doubleday, 1961), 151.

60. Farrer, "Griefs and Consolations," in Farrer, *Love Almighty and Ills Unlimited,* 152.

61. Farrer, "The End of Man," in Farrer, *The End of Man,* 4–5 (also Farrer, *Essential Sermons,* 26). Preached in Pusey House, Oxford, during Hilary Term, 1966, as part of a course on the theme "Christian Faith and Practice."

62. Farrer, *The Triple Victory,* 32.

63. Farrer, "The Legacy," in Farrer, *A Celebration of Faith,* 102 (also Farrer, *Essential Sermons,* 74). Preached in Pusey House Chapel, Oxford, 1968. See John 14–16.

64. Farrer, "Law and Spirit," in Farrer, *Saving Belief,* 125–26 (107–8 in Howatch edition).

65. Austin Farrer, "The Trinity in Whom We Live," *Theology* 56 (September 1953): 326. Originally a radio address, "Meditation for Trinity Sunday," recorded on June 6, 1952, and transmitted on the BBC on June 8, 1952. Recording Number SLO 10356.

66. Ibid., 326.

67. Farrer, "History and the Gospel," in Farrer, *A Celebration of Faith,* 44.

68. Farrer, "Law and Spirit," in Farrer, *Saving Belief,* 129–30 (111–12 in Howatch edition).

69. Ibid., 122 (104 in Howatch edition).

70. Ibid., 132 (114 in Howatch edition).

71. Farrer, "Responsibility for Our Friends," in Farrer, *The Brink of Mystery,* 60 (also Farrer, *Essential Sermons,* 135). Preached in Keble College Chapel, Oxford, 1967.

72. Farrer, "Law and Spirit," in Farrer, *Saving Belief,* 120 (102 in Howatch edition).

73. Farrer, "The Living God," in Farrer, *Words for Life,* 83.

74. Farrer, "The Christian Doctrine of Man," in Jessop et al., *The Christian Understanding of Man,* 211 (also Farrer, *Interpretation and Belief,* 92).

75. Farrer, "Law and Spirit," in Farrer, *Saving Belief,* 132 (114 in Howatch edition).

76. Farrer, "Moving God's Heart," in Farrer, *Words for Life,* 31.

77. Farrer, "Law and Spirit," in Farrer, *Saving Belief,* 132 (114 in Howatch edition).

78. Farrer, "Communion of Faith," in Farrer, *A Faith of Our Own,* 49–50.

79. Farrer, "Responsibility for Our Friends," in Farrer, *The Brink of Mystery,* 60 (also Farrer, *Essential Sermons,* 135).

80. Farrer, "Forgiveness of Sins," in Farrer, *A Faith of Our Own,* 70.

81. Farrer, "Sabbath and Sunday," in Farrer, *A Faith of Our Own,* 86.

82. Farrer, "The Gentleman-Apostle," in Farrer, *Said or Sung,* 45 (also Farrer, *Essential Sermons,* 15). Preached in Trinity College Chapel, Oxford.

83. Farrer, "The Mingling Waters," in Farrer, *A Celebration of Faith,* 206–7. Preached in Trinity College Chapel, Oxford, 1960.

84. Farrer, "Epiphany vi," in Farrer, *The Crown of the Year,* 18.

85. Farrer, "Epiphany iv," in Farrer, *The Crown of the Year,* 16.

86. Farrer, "Sexagesima," in Farrer, *The Crown of the Year,* 20.

87. Farrer, "The Burning-Glass," in Farrer, *Said or Sung,* 109 (also Farrer, *Essential Sermons,* 21).

88. Farrer, "Walking Sacraments," in Farrer, *A Celebration of Faith,* 109 (also Farrer, *Essential Sermons,* 102).

89. Farrer, *The Triple Victory,* 25.

90. Ibid., 33.

91. Farrer, "Forgiveness of Sins," in Farrer, *A Faith of Our Own,* 70.

92. Farrer, "Moving God's Heart," in Farrer, *Words for Life,* 30.

93. Farrer, "A Share of the Family," in Farrer, *A Celebration of Faith,* 106.

94. Farrer, "Eucharist and Church in the New Testament," in Hebert, *The Parish Communion,* 75. Farrer states that the purpose of this essay is to show how this is so.

95. Farrer, "Fish Out of Water," in Farrer, *A Faith of Our Own,* 139 (in Farrer, *Said or Sung,* 120–21).

96. Farrer, "The Hidden Spring," in Farrer, *A Celebration of Faith,* 184 (also Farrer, *Essential Sermons,* 146). Preached in St. Mary the Virgin, Oxford.

97. Farrer, "This Is My Body," in Farrer, *Said or Sung,* 128. In light of the significance of bread as common food, Farrer notes that St. Paul's statement, "Since the loaf is one, we many partakers are one body; for we all partake of the one loaf" (1 Cor. 10:17), was not "saying anything remarkable" from St. Paul's perspective. It was "quite a matter of course" (127–28). Presented to the Eucharistic Congress in the Albert Hall, May 1958.

98. Ibid., 127.

99. Farrer, "Lent vi," in Farrer, *The Crown of the Year,* 27.

100. Farrer, "Lent iv," in Farrer, *The Crown of the Year,* 25.

101. Farrer, *Lord I Believe,* 49.

102. Farrer, "Committed Christians," in Farrer, *Said or Sung,* 146 (also Farrer, *Essential Sermons,* 182).

103. Farrer, "The Body of Christ," in Farrer, *The Crown of the Year,* 71.

104. Ibid., 72.

105. Farrer, "Eucharist and Church in the New Testament," in Hebert, *The Parish Communion,* 92.

106. Farrer, "The Day's Work," in Farrer, *A Celebration of Faith,* 196 (also Farrer, *Essential Sermons,* 111).

107. Farrer, "Assurance," in Farrer, *Said or Sung,* 85 (also Farrer, *Essential Sermons,* 6). Preached in Pusey House, Oxford. See Austin Farrer, "How Do We Know We Have Found Him?" in *Christ and the Christian: A Course of Sermons on Evangelism in the Church Preached in the Chapel of Pusey House, Oxford* (London: A. R. Mowbray, 1956), 23–24.

108. Farrer, "Double Thinking," in Farrer, *A Celebration of Faith,* 26 (also Farrer, *Essential Sermons,* 85).

109. Farrer, "Assurance," in Farrer, *Said or Sung,* 85 (also Farrer, *Essential Sermons,* 6).

110. J. O. F. Murray, *DuBose as a Prophet of Unity* (London: Society for Promoting Christian Knowledge, 1924), 43. (A series of lectures of the DuBose Foundation delivered at the University of the South.) See Slocum, *The Theology of William Porcher DuBose,* 98.

111. William Porcher DuBose, *The Ecumenical Councils,* 2nd ed., vol. 3 of *Ten Epochs of Church History,* ed. John Fulton (Edinburgh: T. & T. Clark, 1897), 29, 321. See Slocum, *The Theology of William Porcher DuBose,* 97–102.

112. Murray, *DuBose as a Prophet of Unity,* 43.

3. The Ultimate Hope

1. *The Book of Common Prayer, and Administration of the Sacraments and Other Rites and Ceremonies of the Church, Together with The Psalter or Psalms of David, according to the Use of the Episcopal Church* (New York: Oxford University Press, 1990), 861.

2. Farrer, "Always Beginning," in Farrer, *A Celebration of Faith,* 165 (also Farrer, *Essential Sermons,* 165). Preached in Keble College Chapel, 1968.

3. Farrer, "Heaven and Hell," in Farrer, *Saving Belief,* 146 (126 in Howatch edition).

4. Ibid., 140–41 (120–21 in Howatch edition).

5. Farrer, "Freedom and Theology," in Farrer, *Reflective Faith,* 168.

6. Farrer, "The Magnet of God," in Farrer, *A Celebration of Faith,* 90.

7. Farrer, "The Christian Doctrine of Man," in Jessop et al., *The Christian Understanding of Man,* 188 (also Farrer, *Interpretation and Belief,* 75).

8. See Robert Boak Slocum, "A Heart for the Future: Reflections on the Christian Hope," in *A Heart for the Future: Writings on the Christian Hope,* ed. Robert Boak Slocum (New York: Church Publishing, 2004), 3.

9. Farrer, *St Matthew and St Mark,* 12–13.

10. Austin Farrer, *A Study in St Mark* (London: Dacre, 1951), 285.

11. Ibid., 230. See Mark 8:27–30.

12. Farrer, "Heaven and Hell," in Farrer, *Saving Belief,* 143 (123 in Howatch edition).

13. Ibid.

14. Farrer, "The Ultimate Hope," in Farrer, *A Celebration of Faith,* 122 (also Farrer, *Essential Sermons,* 203). Preached in St. Andrew's, Headington, on December 22, 1968. This was Farrer's last sermon; it "went out on BBC radio." Curtis, *A Hawk among Sparrows,* 168.

15. 1 Corinthians 13:12a (KJV).

16. Farrer, *Lord I Believe,* 68.

17. Ibid., 78.

18. Farrer, "Always Beginning," in Farrer, *A Celebration of Faith,* 164 (also Farrer, *Essential Sermons,* 165).

19. Farrer, "Heaven and Hell," in Farrer, *Saving Belief,* 141 (121 in Howatch edition).

20. Ibid., 146 (126 in Howatch edition).

21. Farrer, "Into the Hands," in Farrer, *A Celebration of Faith,* 115. Preached in St. Mary's, Primrose Hill, Advent, 1959.

22. Ibid., 115.

23. Farrer, *Lord I Believe,* 73.

24. Farrer, "The Magnet of God," in Farrer, *A Celebration of Faith,* 90.

25. Farrer, "Into the Hands," in Farrer, *A Celebration of Faith,* 116.

26. Farrer, "Eucharist and Church in the New Testament," in Hebert, *The Parish Communion,* 85–86.

27. Farrer, "A Christian's Dilemmas, (1) Submission to God or Mastery of Nature," in Farrer, *A Celebration of Faith,* 125 (also Farrer, *Essential Sermons,* 127).

28. Farrer, "Heaven and Hell," in Farrer, *Saving Belief,* 146 (126 in Howatch edition).

29. Farrer, "The Christian Doctrine of Man," in Jessop et al., *The Christian Understanding of Man,* 202 (also Farrer, *Interpretation and Belief,* 85).

30. Farrer, "Heaven and Hell," in Farrer, *Saving Belief,* 156–57 (136–37 in Howatch edition).

31. Ibid., 157 (137 in Howatch edition).

32. Farrer, *Lord I Believe,* 48–49.

33. See Mark 13:14 and Matthew 24:15.

34. Farrer, *A Study in St Mark,* 141. See Mark 14:50 and Matthew 26:56.

35. Ibid., 285.

36. Farrer, *St Matthew and St Mark,* 104–5. See Mark 13:35–37.

37. Ibid., 105.

38. Ibid.

39. Farrer, "Heaven and Hell," in Farrer, *Saving Belief,* 143–44 (123–24 in Howatch edition).

40. Ibid., 144 (124 in Howatch edition).

41. Ibid., 144–45 (124–25 in Howatch edition).

42. Ibid., 145–46 (125–26 in Howatch edition)

43. Farrer, *Lord I Believe,* 48.

44. Farrer, "The Prior Actuality of God," in Farrer, *Reflective Faith,* 180.

45. Farrer, "Trinity," in Farrer, *The Crown of the Year,* 37.

46. Farrer, "A Father's Begetting," in Farrer, *The End of Man,* 71. Preached on Trinity Sunday, 1961, in Keble College Chapel, Oxford. Also preached at St. Edmund Hall, Oxford, Michaelmas Term, 1963.

47. Farrer, "The Trinity in Whom We Live," *Theology* 56 (September 1953): 326–27. Paul states to the Athenians that in God "we live and move and have our being" (Acts 17:28).

48. Farrer, "Eucharist and Church in the New Testament," in Hebert, *The Parish Communion,* 83.

49. Farrer, *Lord I Believe,* 48.

50. T. S. Eliot, "The Dry Salvages," in *Four Quartets* (San Diego: Harvest/HBJ Books, 1988), 44 (lines 201–2).

51. Edward Yarnold, S.J., *The Awe-Inspiring Rites of Initiation: Baptismal Homilies of the Fourth Century* (Middlegreen, Slough [U.K.]: St Paul Publications, 1971), 44.

52. Farrer, *Lord I Believe,* 48–49.

53. Farrer, *St Matthew and St Mark,* 79. See Mark 4:1–9.

54. Farrer, *A Study in St Mark,* 93. See Mark 6:30–44.

55. Ibid., 94. See Mark 6:41.

56. *Book of Common Prayer,* 860.

57. Farrer, *A Study in St Mark,* 87. See Mark 4:35–5:13 and Exodus 14:5–30.

58. Ibid., 94.

59. Cyril of Jerusalem, "Sermon I, The Prebaptismal Rites," in Yarnold, *The Awe-Inspiring Rites of Initiation,* 69. See Exodus 14.

60. Farrer, "Always Beginning," in Farrer, *A Celebration in Faith*, 165 (also Farrer, *Essential Sermons*, 165).

61. Farrer, "The Painter's Colours," in Farrer, *A Celebration of Faith*, 66 (also Farrer, *Essential Sermons*, 4). Preached in Christ Church Cathedral, Oxford, 1963.

62. Farrer, "The End of Man," in Farrer, *The End of Man*, 4 (also Farrer, *Essential Sermons*, 25). Preached in Pusey House, Oxford, during Hilary Term, 1966, as part of a course on the theme "Christian Faith and Practice."

63. Farrer, "The Window into Heaven: On Making a Retreat," in Farrer, *A Celebration of Faith*, 212. Preached in Keble College Chapel, 1965.

64. Farrer, "The Painter's Colours," in Farrer, *A Celebration of Faith*, 66 (also Farrer, *Essential Sermons*, 4).

65. Farrer, "The End of Man," in Farrer, *The End of Man*, 4 (also Farrer, *Essential Sermons*, 25).

66. Farrer, "The Ultimate Hope," in Farrer, *A Celebration of Faith*, 118–19 (also Farrer, *Essential Sermons*, 200).

67. William Porcher DuBose, *The Reason of Life* (New York: Longmans, Green, 1911), 118.

4. The Problem of Evil

1. Farrer, "The Christian Doctrine of Man," in Jessop et al., *The Christian Understanding of Man*, 197 (also Farrer, *Interpretation and Belief*, 81).

2. Farrer, *Love Almighty and Ills Unlimited*, 26.

3. Farrer, "Lead Us Not into Temptation," in Farrer, *A Celebration of Faith*, 181.

4. Farrer, "Providence and Evil," in Farrer, *Saving Belief*, 49 (37 in Howatch edition). See Matthew 13:24–30.

5. Farrer, "Lead Us Not into Temptation," in Farrer, *A Celebration of Faith*, 182.

6. Simon Oliver, "The Theodicy of Austin Farrer," *Heythrop Journal* 39, no. 3 (1988): 283.

7. Farrer, *Love Almighty and Ills Unlimited*, 30.

8. Ibid.

9. Ibid., 23–24.

10. Ibid., 24.

11. Ibid., 30.

12. Austin Farrer, "Transcendence," radio address, recorded June 29, 1967, and transmitted on the BBC on August 8, 1967, 6, recording number TLN26/RG033D, typescript available in the Keble College Library Archives, used by the kind permission of the Warden and Fellows of Keble College, Oxford; and the Trustees of K. D. Farrer (in Farrer, "Transcendence and 'Radical Theology,'" in Farrer, *Reflective Faith*, 173–74).

13. Farrer, *Love Almighty and Ills Unlimited*, 49.

14. Ibid., 52.

15. Austin Farrer, *A Science of God?* (London: Geoffrey Bles, 1966), 90–91. *A Science of God?* was the bishop of London's Lent book in 1966. It was published in the United States as *God Is Not Dead* (New York: Morehouse-Barlow, 1966).

16. Farrer, *A Science of God?* 91.

17. Farrer, *Love Almighty and Ills Unlimited,* 54.

18. Ibid., 27.

19. Ibid., 27.

20. See ibid., 52.

21. Farrer, *A Science of God?* 87–88.

22. Farrer, *Love Almighty and Ills Unlimited,* 56.

23. Ibid., 47–48.

24. Ibid., 70.

25. Ibid., 56.

26. Ibid., 148.

27. Ibid., 149.

28. Ibid.

29. Ibid., 18. For example, Job's friend Eliphaz asks him, rhetorically, "Is not your wickedness great?" and states, "There is no end to your iniquities" (Job 22:5). Job maintains his innocence.

30. Ibid., 18.

31. C. S. Lewis describes his experience of grief after Joy's death in *A Grief Observed* (London and Boston: Faber and Faber, 1961). Ann Loades believes it is "credible" that Farrer "has Lewis's experience and work in mind" in "Griefs and Consolations," the last chapter of *Love Almighty and Ills Unlimited.* Ann Loades, "The Vitality of Tradition: Austin Farrer and Friends," in Hein and Henderson, *Captured by the Crucified,* 35.

32. Austin Farrer, "The Christian Apologist," in *Light on C. S. Lewis,* ed. Jocelyn Gibb (London: Geoffrey Bles, 1965), 32. Farrer once commented in a letter that if Lewis' grief over Joy's death killed him by weakening his heart due to "prolonged continued strain," it also "completed him," and that "in his last days he was a magnificent man." Austin Farrer to Martyn Skinner, December 10, 1963, in Letters from Austin Farrer and Katharine Farrer to Martyn Skinner folder, box 4, Farrer Papers. Used with the kind permission of the Trustees of the K. D. Farrer Trust.

33. Farrer, *Love Almighty and Ills Unlimited,* 148.

34. Ibid., 149.

35. Ibid., 148.

36. Ibid., 92–93.

37. Farrer, *Lord I Believe,* 63.

38. Farrer, *Love Almighty and Ills Unlimited,* 164.

39. Job 2:9.

40. Farrer, *Love Almighty and Ills Unlimited,* 164.

41. Ibid., 164–65.

42. William Stringfellow, *An Ethic for Christians and Other Aliens in a Strange Land* (Waco, Texas: Word Books, 1973), 118–19. See Robert Boak Slocum, "William Stringfellow and the Christian Witness against Death," in *Prophet of Justice, Prophet of Life: Essays on William Stringfellow,* ed. Robert Boak Slocum (New York: Church Publishing, 1997), 31.

43. Stringfellow, *An Ethic for Christians and Other Aliens,* 138.

44. Farrer, *Love Almighty and Ills Unlimited,* 93.

45. Ibid., 150–51.

46. Ibid., 93.

47. Ibid., 153.

48. Ibid., 152.

49. Farrer, "Lead Us Not into Temptation," in Farrer, *A Celebration of Faith,* 181.

50. Farrer, "The Commander's Love," in Farrer, *A Celebration of Faith,* 173 (also Farrer, *Essential Sermons,* 151).

51. Farrer, *Love Almighty and Ills Unlimited,* 151.

52. Ibid.

53. Ibid., 152.

54. Ibid., 151–52.

55. Ibid., 151.

56. Ibid., 152–53.

57. Farrer, "Providence and Evil," in Farrer, *Saving Belief,* 46–48 (34–35 in Howatch edition).

58. Farrer, *Love Almighty and Ills Unlimited,* 58.

59. Oliver, "The Theodicy of Austin Farrer," 284.

60. Austin Farrer, editor's introduction, in *Theodicy: Essays on the Goodness of God, the Freedom of Man, and the Origin of Evil,* by G. W. Leibniz, ed. Austin Farrer, trans. E. M. Huggard from C. J. Gerhardt's edition of the *Collected Philosophical Works, 1875–1890* (LaSalle, Ill.: Open Court, 1985), 31–32.

61. Farrer, "Providence and Evil," in Farrer, *Saving Belief,* 58 (46 in Howatch edition).

62. Ibid., 48 (36 in Howatch edition).

63. Farrer, *Love Almighty and Ills Unlimited,* 55.

64. Ibid., 64.

65. Farrer, "Providence and Evil," in Farrer, *Saving Belief,* 53 (41 in Howatch edition).

66. Ibid., 58 (46 in Howatch edition). See Matthew 13:24–30.

67. Farrer, *A Science of God?* 87.

68. Ibid., 89.

69. Farrer, "Providence and Evil," in Farrer, *Saving Belief,* 55 (43 in Howatch edition).

70. Ibid., 54 (42 in Howatch edition).

71. Austin Farrer, *A Rebirth of Images: The Making of St. John's Apocalypse* (Glasgow: University Press, 1949; Albany: State University of New York Press, 1986), 24.

72. Farrer, "Providence and Evil," in Farrer, *Saving Belief,* 57 (45 in Howatch edition). See Mark 14:32–42.

73. Ibid.

74. Ibid., 54 (42 in Howatch edition).

75. Farrer, "Commemoration of Charles Linnell, 1915–1964," in Farrer, *A Celebration of Faith,* 216. Preached in Keble College Chapel.

76. Hebblethwaite, "Austin Farrer's Concept of Divine Providence," 545.

77. Farrer, "Lead Us Not into Temptation," in Farrer, *A Celebration of Faith,* 182.

78. Farrer, *A Science of God?* 90.

79. Farrer, *Love Almighty and Ills Unlimited,* 166.

80. Ibid., 166–67.

81. Farrer, *Finite and Infinite,* 34.

82. Loades made this suggestion at the Captured by the Crucified conference in honor of the centenary of Farrer's birth. This conference was held at the St. James Center for Spiritual Formation in Baton Rouge, Louisiana, November 4–7, 2004.

83. Curtis, *A Hawk among Sparrows,* 144.

84. Farrer, "The Country Doctor," in Farrer, *Said or Sung,* 28 (also Farrer, *Essential Sermons,* 204). Preached in Christ Church Cathedral, Oxford, on Christmas Day.

85. Farrer, "The Trinity in Whom We Live," 327.

86. Ann Loades, "Austin Farrer on *Love Almighty,*" in Eaton and Loades, *For God and Clarity,* 107.

87. Farrer, *Lord I Believe,* 92.

88. Farrer, "Lead Us Not into Temptation," in Farrer, *A Celebration of Faith,* 183.

89. Farrer, *Finite and Infinite,* 300.

5. Transforming Images

1. Farrer, "Lecture III," in Farrer, *The Glass of Vision,* 44.

2. Farrer, *A Rebirth of Images,* 13.

3. Austin Farrer, "Important Hypotheses Reconsidered, VIII. Typology," *Expository Times* 67 (May 1956): 229.

4. Carl G. Jung, "Foreword to the Fourth (Swiss) Edition (September 1950)," in Carl G. Jung, *Symbols of Transformation: An Analysis of the Prelude to a Case of Schizophrenia,* 2nd ed., trans. R. F. C. Hull, vol. 5 of the *Collected Works of C. G. Jung* (Princeton, N.J.: Princeton University Press, 1967), xxiv.

5. Carl G. Jung, "Foreword to the Second (German) Edition (November, 1924)," in Jung, *Symbols of Transformation,* xxviii.

6. Jung, "Foreword to the Fourth (Swiss) Edition," xxiv.

7. Carl G. Jung, *Man and His Symbols* (Garden City, N.Y.: Doubleday, 1964), 102.

8. Carl G. Jung, "Foreword to the Third (German) Edition (November, 1937)," in Jung, *Symbols of Transformation*, xxvii.

9. Travis Du Priest, "Spirit: Inner Witness and Guardian of the Soul," in *Engaging the Spirit: Essays on the Life and Theology of the Holy Spirit*, ed. Robert Boak Slocum (New York: Church Publishing, 2001), 30.

10. Farrer, "Lecture VI," in Farrer, *The Glass of Vision*, 108.

11. Farrer, "Lecture VIII," in Farrer, *The Glass of Vision*, 148.

12. Farrer, "Lecture VI," in Farrer, *The Glass of Vision*, 110.

13. Rodger Forsman, "Revelation and Understanding: A Defence of Tradition," in *Hermeneutics, the Bible and Literary Criticism*, ed. Ann Loades and Michael McLain (New York: St. Martin's Press, 1992), 65.

14. Ingolf Dalferth, "The Stuff of Revelation: Austin Farrer's Doctrine of Inspired Images," in Loades and McLain, *Hermeneutics, the Bible and Literary Criticism*, 73.

15. Stephen Platten, "Diaphanous Thought: Spirituality and Theology in the Work of Austin Farrer," *Anglican Theological Review* 69, no. 1 (January 1987): 32. Platten was canon residentiary of Portsmouth Cathedral in England. He was also diocesan director of ordinands and lay-ministry adviser.

16. Platten, "Diaphanous Thought," 32–33. The organization was founded in 1941 by Elia Estelle ("Stella") Aldwinckle to provide the University of Oxford with an open forum for discussion of intellectual difficulties concerning religion, especially Christianity. Hooper, *C. S. Lewis*, 617–18. Aldwinckle edited five volumes of the *Socratic Digest*, 1942–52.

17. Dorothy L. Sayers, *The Mind of the Maker* (New York: Harcourt, Brace, 1941), 21–22.

18. Ibid., 21–22. See Exodus 20:4.

19. Farrer, *A Rebirth of Images*, 14.

20. Farrer, "Lecture III," in Farrer, *The Glass of Vision*, 42.

21. Farrer, "Lecture VIII," in Farrer, *The Glass of Vision*, 134.

22. Farrer, "Lecture III," in Farrer, *The Glass of Vision*, 51.

23. Ibid., 51–52.

24. Farrer, "Lecture VII," in Farrer, *The Glass of Vision*, 113.

25. Farrer, "Lecture IV," in Farrer, *The Glass of Vision*, 61.

26. Farrer, "Lecture III," in Farrer, *The Glass of Vision*, 44–45.

27. Ibid., 45.

28. Ibid., 44.

29. Ibid., 44, 51.

30. Ibid., 43–44.

31. Ibid.

32. Emmet, *The Nature of Metaphysical Thinking*, 106.

33. Farrer, "Lecture IV," in Farrer, *The Glass of Vision*, 57.

34. Farrer, "Lecture III," in Farrer, *The Glass of Vision*, 56.

35. Ibid., 53–54.

36. Ibid., 50–51.

37. Ibid., 43.

38. Ibid.

39. Ibid.

40. Ibid., 52–53.

41. Ibid., 54.

42. Ibid., 46–47.

43. Ibid., 47–48. See Isaiah 11:1–2.

44. Ibid.

45. Ibid., 48.

46. Ibid., 48–49. See Revelation 5:6 and Isaiah 11:1–2.

47. Ibid., 49–50. See Revelation 4:5.

48. Farrer, "Lecture VIII," in Farrer, *The Glass of Vision*, 136.

49. Ibid., 133.

50. Ibid., 136.

51. Farrer, "Lecture VI," in Farrer, *The Glass of Vision*, 111. See John 1:1–14.

52. Ibid.

53. Farrer, "Lecture VIII," in Farrer, *The Glass of Vision*, 144–46.

54. Farrer, "Lecture III," in Farrer, *The Glass of Vision*, 50–51.

55. John Macquarrie, *Jesus Christ in Modern Thought* (London and Philadelphia: SCM Press and Trinity Press International, 1990), 119. Macquarrie cites Bultmann's statement that "just as all the waters of the earth point to the one living water, and as all bread on the earth points to the one bread of life, and as all day-light points to the light of the world, just as every earthly vine is contrasted with the 'true' vine, so too every shepherd in the world is contrasted with the 'good' shepherd." Rudolf Bultmann, *The Gospel of John: A Commentary,* trans. G. R. Beasley-Murray, gen. ed., R. W. N. Hoare and J. K. Riches (Philadelphia: Westminster Press, 1971), 364. See John 4:5–26, 6:35–41, 8:12, 15:1–6, and 10:1–16.

56. Farrer, "Lecture VIII," in Farrer, *The Glass of Vision*, 134.

57. Ibid.

58. Farrer, *A Rebirth of Images*, 14.

59. Farrer, "Lecture VIII," in Farrer, *The Glass of Vision*, 135.

60. Ibid.

61. Farrer, "Lecture VI," in Farrer, *The Glass of Vision*, 109.

62. A. M. Farrer, "The Ministry in the New Testament," in *The Apostolic Ministry: Essays on the History and the Doctrine of Episcopacy,* ed. Kenneth E. Kirk (London: Hodder & Stoughton, 1946), 116.

63. Farrer, "Lecture VI," in Farrer, *The Glass of Vision*, 108–9.

64. Ibid., 109.

65. Farrer, *A Rebirth of Images*, 15.

66. Ibid.

67. Ibid., 17.

68. Ibid., 17–18. See Revelation 5:6 and Exodus 3:1–6.

69. Ibid., 106–7. See Genesis 22:1–19 and Revelation 5:1–6.

70. Ibid., 110.

71. Ibid., 110–11. See Genesis 4:10, in which the Lord addresses Cain after he has murdered Abel: "'What have you done? Listen; your brother's blood is crying out to me from the ground!'"

72. The Revelation describes "a great multitude that no one could count, from every nation, from all tribes and peoples and languages, standing before the throne and before the Lamb, robed in white, with palm branches in their hands." One of the elders states, "'These are they who have come out of the great ordeal; they have washed their robes and made them white in the blood of the Lamb'" (Rev. 7:9, 13–14). This vision precedes the opening of the seventh seal of the heavenly scroll.

73. Farrer, *The Revelation of St. John the Divine*, v.

74. Ibid., 94.

75. Ibid., 112.

76. Ibid., 218.

77. William Blake, *Jerusalem*, in *The Poetry and Prose of William Blake*, ed. David V. Erdman (Garden City, N.Y.: Doubleday, 1965), 255 (chap. 4, 98.24–27).

78. Hieromonk Alexander Golitzin, "'I See Your Bridal Chamber Adorned': An Eastern Orthodox Reflection on the Eschaton in Light of the 'Pattern' of Divine Worship," in Slocum, *A Heart for the Future*, 86.

79. Farrer, "Mary, Scripture, and Tradition," in Mascall and Box, *The Blessed Virgin Mary*, 35 (also Farrer, *Interpretation and Belief*, 108–9). See Luke 1:5–38.

80. Ibid., 35–36 (also Farrer, *Interpretation and Belief*, 109). See Acts 9:10–22 (revelations to Saul and Ananias).

81. "Mary, Scripture, and Tradition," in Mascall and Box, *The Blessed Virgin Mary*, 50–52 (also Farrer, *Interpretation and Belief*, 123–25). The woman "gave birth to a son, a male child, who is to rule all the nations with a rod of iron." He was "snatched away and taken to God and to his throne; and the woman fled into the wilderness, where she has a place prepared by God, so that there she can be nourished for one thousand two hundred sixty days" (Rev. 12:5–6).

6. Poetical Inspiration and Literary Interpretation

1. Farrer, "Important Hypotheses Reconsidered, VIII. Typology," 228.

2. Farrer, "Lecture VIII," in Farrer, *The Glass of Vision*, 136.

3. Ibid., 148.

4. Farrer, *The Revelation of St. John the Divine*, 28. Farrer states that "it was equally natural that the process should issue in descriptions of vision, since vision was what the old prophets' written words depicted."

5. Farrer, *A Rebirth of Images*, 20.

6. Ibid., 21.

7. Ibid., 130.

8. Ibid., 18.

9. Ibid., 25.

10. Farrer, "Lecture III," in Farrer, *The Glass of Vision*, 45. See Farrer, "Lecture III," in Farrer, *The Glass of Vision*, 51.

11. Farrer, "Lecture VII," in Farrer, *The Glass of Vision*, 128.

12. Ibid., 129.

13. Ibid., 127.

14. Ibid., 129.

15. Hefling, "Farrer's Scriptural Divinity," in Hein and Henderson, *Captured by the Crucified*, 149.

16. Farrer, "Lecture VIII," in Farrer, *The Glass of Vision*, 136. I have drawn quotations of Mark 16:1–8 from the New Revised Standard Version of the Bible. Farrer states that the twelve verses at the end of Mark 16 "were added by a competent scribe to round the story off and bring it into parallel with the conclusions of the other gospels."

17. Farrer, "Lecture VIII," in Farrer, *The Glass of Vision*, 136–37. H. G. Dickinson wrote to Katharine Farrer shortly after Austin's death to say that "I like to think of him meeting S. Mark and having the truth at last, and that he is caught up in the central heart of love which he taught me to know [and] believe in." H. G. Dickinson to Katharine Farrer, December 29, 1968, in Letters from Various Friends I folder, box 4, Farrer Papers. Used with the kind permission of the Trustees of the K. D. Farrer Trust.

18. Farrer, *St Matthew and St Mark*, 144.

19. Farrer, "Lecture VIII," in Farrer, *The Glass of Vision*, 138–39.

20. Ibid., 145.

21. Ibid., 140.

22. Farrer, *A Study in St Mark*, 174.

23. Ibid., 180–81.

24. Frank Kermode, *The Genesis of Secrecy: On the Interpretation of Narrative*, Charles Eliot Norton Lectures, 1977–78 (Cambridge: Harvard University Press, 1979), 72. Kermode notes the "double pattern of events before and after the Crucifixion" identified by Farrer. Before the crucifixion, "Jesus said he would go to Galilee; spoke of the anointing; gave to the disciples at the Last Supper a sacramental body which should have made it clear to them that the walling up of a physical body was unimportant. The disciples fled before the Crucifixion, the women after it" (70).

25. David Rhoads, preface to *Mark as Story: An Introduction to the Narrative of a Gospel*, by David Rhoads and Donald Michie (Philadelphia: Fortress Press, 1982), xv. Rhoads and Michie taught at Carthage College in Kenosha, Wisconsin.

26. Rhoads and Michie, *Mark as Story*, 1, 3.

27. Ibid., 5.

28. Richard A. Edwards, *Matthew's Narrative Portrait of Disciples: How the Text-Connoted Reader Is Informed* (Harrisburg, Pa.: Trinity Press International, 1997), 6. He provides an extensive footnote that lists the primary books for understanding narrative

criticism (5n4). Edwards was associate professor in the Department of Theology at Marquette University in Milwaukee, Wisconsin.

29. Ibid., 7.

30. Ibid., 11.

31. Ibid., 1.

32. Ibid., v, 9, 15.

33. Jeffrey Peterson, "A Pioneer Narrative Critic and His Synoptic Hypothesis: Austin Farrer and Gospel Interpretation," *Society of Biblical Literature 2000 Seminar Papers* 39 (2000): 661–62, 670–71.

34. Farrer, "Lecture VIII," in Farrer, *The Glass of Vision,* 140.

35. Ibid., 140–41. See Mark 14:3–52.

36. Ibid., 141. See Mark 15:43–16:8.

37. Ibid.

38. Ibid., 142.

39. Ibid., 144–45.

40. Ibid., 145. See Genesis 37:15–24, 39:6–20, and 45:1–3.

41. Ibid., 145–46.

42. David Jasper, *Coleridge as Poet and Religious Thinker* (Allison Park, Pa.: Pickwick Publications, 1985), 145. Jasper states that the "debate" over Farrer's method in *The Glass of Vision,* was "renewed in the recent exchanges" between Frank Kermode and Helen Gardner (145). See Kermode, *The Genesis of Secrecy;* and Helen Gardner, *In Defence of the Imagination* (Cambridge: Harvard University Press, 1982).

43. Helen Gardner, *The Business of Criticism* (Oxford: Clarendon Press, 1959), 108–11. *The Business of Criticism* includes two sets of lectures by Gardner. The second series, "The Limits of Literary Criticism," was given at King's College, Newcastle, in 1956, in response to the invitation of the University of Durham for her to deliver the Riddell Memorial Lectures for 1956. The second of these lectures was "The Poetry of St. Mark." Gardner's 1956 Riddell Memorial Lectures were published separately as *The Limits of Literary Criticism: Reflections on the Interpretation of Poetry and Scripture* (London: Oxford University Press, 1956). Dame Helen Gardner was Merton Professor of Literature at Oxford University.

44. Gardner, *The Business of Criticism,* 113–14.

45. Ibid., 118–19.

46. Ibid., 120–21.

47. Ibid., 122, 126.

48. Gardner, *In Defence of the Imagination,* 114.

49. H. D. Lewis, *Our Experience of God* (London: George Allen & Unwin; New York: Macmillan, 1959), 136–37. Lewis was professor of history and philosophy of religion in the University of London and general editor of the Muirhead Library of Philosophy.

50. Ibid., 137–38.

51. Ibid., 138.

52. Ibid., 138–39.

53. Farrer, "Inspiration: Poetical and Divine," in Farrer, *Interpretation and Belief,* 39. This essay originally appeared in F. F. Bruce, ed., *Promise and Fulfilment: Essays Presented to Professor S. H. Hooke, in Celebration of His Ninetieth Birthday, 21st January 1964, by Members of the Society for Old Testament Study and Others* (Edinburgh: T. & T. Clark, 1963), 91–105.

54. Farrer, "Inspiration: Poetical and Divine," in Farrer, *Interpretation and Belief,* 39.

55. Ibid., 44–45.

56. Ibid., 46–47.

57. Ibid., 49. See Revelation 5–8.

58. Ibid., 51.

59. Ibid., 53.

60. Farrer, "On Looking below the Surface," in Farrer, *Interpretation and Belief,* 54. This was Farrer's Presidential Address to the Oxford Society of Historical Theology, October 22, 1959. It was reprinted from the *Proceedings of the Oxford Society of Historical Theology* (1959–60): 3–18.

61. Farrer, "On Looking below the Surface," in Farrer, *Interpretation and Belief,* 54–55.

62. Ibid., 56–57.

63. Ibid., 58.

64. See Farrer, "Lecture III," in Farrer, *The Glass of Vision,* 43–56, and my discussion of "Image and Event" in this chapter.

65. Farrer, "On Looking below the Surface," in Farrer, *Interpretation and Belief,* 60.

66. Farrer, "Important Hypotheses Reconsidered, VIII. Typology," 228.

67. Farrer, "On Looking below the Surface," in Farrer, *Interpretation and Belief,* 60–63.

68. Ibid., 65.

7. Divine Action and Human Freedom

1. Farrer, *The Freedom of the Will,* 330.

2. Edward Hugh Henderson, "The God Who Undertakes Us," in Hein and Henderson, *Captured by the Crucified,* 85–86.

3. Farrer, "The Christian Doctrine of Man," in Jessop et al., *The Christian Understanding of Man,* 210 (also Farrer, *Interpretation and Belief,* 91).

4. Austin Farrer, "How Was Jesus Divine?" *Socratic Digest* 1 (June 1943): 24.

5. Farrer, "Lecture II," in Farrer, *The Glass of Vision,* 32–33.

6. Farrer, "Grace and Freewill," in Farrer, *Faith and Speculation,* 66. Chapters 4–6 ("Grace and Freewill," "Nature and Creation," and "Revelation and History") reflect the "substance" of Farrer's 1964 Deems Lectures at New York University. Austin Farrer, preface to Farrer, *Faith and Speculation,* v. A portion of "Grace and Freewill" (60–67) appears in Owen C. Thomas, ed., *God's Activity in the World: The Contemporary Problem,* American Academy of Religion Studies in Religion no. 31 (Chico, Calif.: Scholars Press, 1983), 195–200.

7. Farrer, "Revelation and History," in Farrer, *Faith and Speculation*, 98.

8. Farrer, "Spiritual Science," in Farrer, *Faith and Speculation*, 36.

9. Farrer, "Lecture II," in Farrer, *The Glass of Vision*, 33.

10. Henderson, "The God Who Undertakes Us," in Hein and Henderson, *Captured by the Crucified*, 67.

11. Farrer, "Spiritual Science," in Farrer, *Faith and Speculation*, 47.

12. Farrer, "Grace and Freewill," in Farrer, *Faith and Speculation*, 66.

13. Farrer, "Transcendence," 10; Farrer, "Transcendence and 'Radical Theology,'" in Farrer, *Reflective Faith*, 176.

14. Farrer, "The Christian Doctrine of Man," in Jessop et al., *The Christian Understanding of Man*, 204 (also Farrer, *Interpretation and Belief*, 87).

15. Farrer, "Grace and Resurrection," in Farrer, *A Celebration of Faith*, 149 (also Farrer, *Essential Sermons*, 139).

16. Martin Luther, *The Bondage of the Will*, trans. Philip S. Watson in collaboration with Benjamin Drewery, in vol. 33 of *Luther's Works*, ed. Philip S. Watson, gen. ed., Helmut T. Lehmann (Philadelphia: Fortress Press, 1972), 243. Luther wrote *The Bondage of the Will* in 1525.

17. Farrer, *The Freedom of the Will*, 310.

18. Farrer, "Anima Mundi," in Farrer, *Faith and Speculation*, 142.

19. Farrer, *Faith and Speculation*, 172.

20. Farrer, "Grace and Freewill," in Farrer, *Faith and Speculation*, 66.

21. Ibid.

22. Farrer, "Lecture II," in Farrer, *The Glass of Vision*, 33.

23. Farrer, "Lecture III," in Farrer, *The Glass of Vision*, 39.

24. Farrer, "Transcendence," 9; Farrer, "Transcendence and 'Radical Theology,'" 176. Similarly, Farrer states that "God not only makes the world, he makes it make itself." Farrer, "Providence and Evil," in Farrer, *Saving Belief*, 51 (39 in Howatch edition). See Henderson, "The God Who Undertakes Us," in Hein and Henderson, *Captured by the Crucified*, 91.

25. Farrer, "Grace and Freewill," in Farrer, *Faith and Speculation*, 67.

26. Henderson, "The God Who Undertakes Us," in Hein and Henderson, *Captured by the Crucified*, 85.

27. Farrer, "Grace and the Human Will," in Farrer, *Reflective Faith*, 199. "Grace and the Human Will" was originally read by Farrer to the Metaphysicals around 1964. Farrer, "Grace and the Human Will," 192n. Charles Conti states that Farrer "was a founder member of the Metaphysicals, an informal society of Oxford dons responsible for publishing *Faith and Logic,* to which he was a contributor." Conti, "Editor's Preface," in Farrer, *Reflective Faith*, vii. See Basil Mitchell, ed., *Faith and Logic: Oxford Essays in Philosophical Theology* (London: George Allen & Unwin, 1957).

28. The Jewish writer Martin Buber distinguished *I-Thou* relations, "which are 'personal,' and *I-It* relations, which are impersonal," so that an *I-Thou* relation exists between two "active subjects" or persons, and "it is something which is *mutual* and *reciprocal.*" Alister E. McGrath, ed., *The Christian Theology Reader*, 2nd ed. (Oxford:

Blackwell Publishing, 2001), 445. Buber states that "relation is only possible between *I* and *Thou*." Martin Buber, *I and Thou*, 2nd ed., trans. Ronald Gregor Smith (New York: Charles Scribner's Sons, 1958), 78. "Marriage, for instance, will never be given new life except by that out of which true marriage always arises, the revealing by two people of the *Thou* to one another." Buber, *I and Thou*, 45–46.

29. Farrer, *A Science of God?* 123.

30. Thomas Aquinas, *Summa Theologica*, trans. Fathers of the English Dominican Province, 5 vols. (Westminster, Md.: Christian Classics, 1981), 58, 62 (pt. 1, q. 12, art. 12 and pt. 1, q. 13, art. 2, obj. 3).

31. Farrer, *A Science of God?* 123.

32. Ibid., 125.

33. Ibid., 76.

34. Sayers, *The Mind of the Maker*, 52.

35. Ibid., 67.

36. Ibid., 138.

37. Farrer, "The Potter's Clay," in Farrer, *Said and Sung*, 80 (also Farrer, *Essential Sermons*, 17). See Jeremiah 18:1–11.

38. Ibid., 80–81 (also Farrer, *Essential Sermons*, 17–18).

39. Ibid., 81 (also Farrer, *Essential Sermons*, 18).

40. Farrer, "Creed and History," in Farrer, *Saving Belief*, 61.

41. Farrer, "Law and Spirit," in Farrer, *Saving Belief*, 124 (106 in Howatch edition).

42. Farrer, "The Spirit and the Name," in Farrer, *Words for Life*, 72.

43. Farrer, *A Science of God?* 107.

44. Ibid., 99.

45. Ibid., 110.

46. Ibid., 108. See Matthew 4:5–7. Jesus rejects Satan's temptation, saying, "Again it is written, 'Do not put the Lord your God to the test.'"

47. Matthew 4:7.

48. Farrer, *A Science of God?* 109.

49. Farrer, "Grace and Freewill," in Farrer, *Faith and Speculation*, 56.

50. John Booty, "An Elizabethan Addresses Modern Anglicanism: Richard Hooker and Theological Issues at the End of the Twentieth Century," *Anglican Theological Review* 71, no. 1 (Winter 1989): 14. See John E. Booty, "Richard Hooker," in *The Spirit of Anglicanism*, ed. William J. Wolf (Wilton, Conn.: Morehouse-Barlow, 1979), 17–20. See Robert B. Slocum, "An Answering Heart: Reflections on Saving Participation," *Anglican Theological Review* 84, no. 4 (Fall 2002): 1009–15.

51. Richard Hooker, *The Folger Library Edition of the Works of Richard Hooker*, vol. 2, *Of the Laws of Ecclesiastical Polity*, ed. W. Speed Hill (Cambridge: Belknap Press of Harvard University Press, 1977), 239.

52. Farrer, *A Science of God?* 109.

53. Ibid., 108.

54. Farrer, "Grace and Freewill," in Farrer, *Faith and Speculation*, 57.

55. Farrer, *The Freedom of the Will,* 330.

56. Ibid., 312.

57. Farrer, *A Science of God?* 107.

58. W. Mark Richardson, "A Look at Austin Farrer's Theory of Agency," in *Human and Divine Agency: Anglican, Catholic, and Lutheran Perspectives,* ed. F. Michael McLain and W. Mark Richardson (Lanham, Md.: University Press of America, 1999), 144.

59. Henderson, "The God Who Undertakes Us," in Hein and Henderson, *Captured by the Crucified,* 81.

60. Farrer, *A Science of God?* 111.

61. Ibid.

62. Farrer, "Liberty and Theology," in Farrer, *The Freedom of the Will,* 315.

63. Farrer, "Grace and Freewill," in Farrer, *Faith and Speculation,* 57.

64. Ibid., 65.

65. Ibid., 66.

66. Farrer, *A Science of God?* 108.

67. Farrer, "Grace and Freewill," in Farrer, *Faith and Speculation,* 66.

68. Farrer, *A Science of God?* 108.

69. Farrer, "Grace and Freewill," in Farrer, *Faith and Speculation,* 65.

70. Farrer, *A Science of God?* 114.

71. Ibid., 114–15.

72. Ibid., 118.

73. Ibid., 107.

74. Ibid., 114.

75. Ibid., 114. See Luke 16:19–31.

76. Ibid., 113.

77. Farrer, *Faith and Speculation,* 171.

78. Farrer, *A Science of God?* 113–14. See Matthew 26:51–53, Matthew 26:63–64, Mark 14:61–62, Mark 15:23, Luke 22:49–51, Luke 22:66–71, Luke 23:34, John 18:10–11, and John 18:33–38.

79. Ibid., 114.

80. Ibid., 127. See Acts 17:28.

81. DuBose, *The Reason of Life,* 78.

82. See Slocum, *The Theology of William Porcher DuBose,* 109.

83. Farrer, *A Science of God?* 127.

84. Martin Luther King Jr., "The Answer to a Perplexing Question," in *Strength to Love* (Philadelphia: Fortress Press, 1981), 134–35.

85. Jerry H. Gill, "Divine Action as Mediated," *Harvard Theological Review* 80, no. 3 (1987): 370.

86. Hebblethwaite, "Austin Farrer's Concept of Divine Providence," 545–46.

87. Farrer, "Grace and the Human Will," in Farrer, *Reflective Faith,* 192.

88. DuBose, *The Reason of Life,* 263.

89. Farrer, "Grace and the Human Will," in Farrer, *Reflective Faith,* 199.

90. Farrer, "A Share of the Family," in Farrer, *A Celebration of Faith,* 104 (also Farrer, *Essential Sermons,* 174).

91. Robert M. Cooper, "This Body of Hope," in Slocum, *A Heart for the Future,* 39.

92. John Macmurray, *Persons in Relation* (Atlantic Highlands, N.J.: Humanities Press, 1991), 211–12. *Persons in Relation,* based on Macmurray's 1953–54 Gifford Lectures at the University of Glasgow, was first published in 1961. The lectures were titled "The Form of the Personal." *Persons in Relation* was the second volume based on these lectures, following *The Self as Agent,* which was first published in 1957. See Robert B. Slocum, "Kingdom Come: Preliminaries for a Relational Theology of Hope," *Anglican Theological Review* 82, no. 3 (Summer 2000): 571–73.

93. Macmurray, *Persons in Relation,* 28–29. See Acts 17:28.

94. Ibid., 211.

95. John Macmurray, *A Challenge to the Churches: Religion and Democracy* (London: Kegan Paul, Trench, Trubner, 1941), 16.

96. John Macquarrie, *Christology Revisited* (Harrisburg, Pa.: Trinity Press International, 1998), 94.

97. Macquarrie, *Christology Revisited,* 94. Macquarrie mentions that this phrase "can be found in Buber but was actually in use at least from the time of Feuerbach."

98. Macmurray, *Persons in Relation,* 28.

99. Macquarrie, *Christology Revisited,* 94.

100. Ibid., 94–95.

101. Farrer, "Grace and the Human Will," in Farrer, *Reflective Faith,* 199.

102. Henderson, "The God Who Undertakes Us," in Hein and Henderson, *Captured by the Crucified,* 85.

103. Farrer, "How Was Jesus Divine?" 24.

104. Farrer, "Grace and the Human Will," in Farrer, *Reflective Faith,* 199.

Works Cited

Archival Sources

Austin Farrer Papers. Modern Papers and John Johnson Reading Room. Department of Special Collections and Western Manuscripts. New Bodleian Library. University of Oxford.

Works by Austin Farrer

"Analogy." In *Twentieth Century Encyclopedia of Religious Knowledge: An Extension of the New Schaff-Herzog Encyclopedia of Religious Knowledge,* edited by Lefferts Augustine Loetscher, 1:38–40. Grand Rapids, Mich.: Baker Book House, 1955. This essay also appears as "Theology and Analogy 1, the Concept of Analogy" in Farrer, *Reflective Faith,* 64–68.

Austin Farrer, the Essential Sermons. Edited by Leslie Houlden. London: SPCK; Cambridge, Mass.: Cowley, 1991 (hereafter *Essential Sermons*).

Bible Sermons: A Course Preached in the Chapel of Pusey House, Oxford, by Christopher Evans and Austin Farrer. London: A. R. Mowbray, 1963. Especially pp. 31–57.

The Brink of Mystery. Edited by Charles C. Conti. London: SPCK, 1976.

A Celebration of Faith: Communications, Mostly to Students. Edited by Leslie Houlden. London: Hodder and Stoughton, 1970.

"The Christian Apologist." In *Light on C. S. Lewis,* edited by Jocelyn Gibb, 23–43. London: Geoffrey Bles, 1965.

"The Christian Doctrine of Man." In *The Christian Understanding of Man,* edited by T. E. Jessop et al., 179–213. The Church, Community, and State series, vol. 2. London: George Allen & Unwin, 1938. Also in Farrer, *Interpretation and Belief,* 69–94.

The Crown of the Year: Weekly Paragraphs for the Holy Sacrament. Westminster: Dacre Press, 1952.

Editor's introduction. In *Theodicy: Essays on the Goodness of God, the Freedom of Man, and the Origin of Evil,* by G. W. Leibniz, 7–47. LaSalle, Ill.: Open Court, 1985.

The End of Man. Edited by Charles C. Conti. London: SPCK, 1973.

"Eucharist and Church in the New Testament." In *The Parish Communion: A Book of Essays,* edited by A. G. Hebert, 75–94. London: Society for Promoting Christian Knowledge; New York: Macmillan, 1937.

"The Everyday Use of the Bible." In *The Bible and the Christian: A Course of Sermons on the Bible Preached in the Chapel of Pusey House, Oxford*, 55–60. London: A. R. Mowbray, 1957.

Faith and Speculation: An Essay in Philosophical Theology Containing the Deems Lectures Delivered at New York University in 1964. New York: New York University Press; London: Adam & Charles Black, 1967. Chapters 4–6 reflect the "substance" of Farrer's 1964 Deems Lectures at New York University.

A Faith of Our Own. Cleveland: World Publishing, 1960.

Finite and Infinite: A Philosophical Essay. 2nd ed. 1943. Reprint, Westminster: Dacre, 1959. Seabury paperback edition published in New York, 1979.

The Freedom of the Will. New York: Charles Scribner's Sons, 1958. An enlargement of Farrer's Gifford Lectures delivered in the University of Edinburgh, 1957.

The Glass of Vision. Westminster: Dacre Press, 1948. The book consists of Farrer's eight Bampton Lectures for 1948.

God Is Not Dead. New York: Morehouse-Barlow, 1966. Published in Great Britain as *A Science of God?*

"How Do We Know We Have Found Him?" In *Christ and the Christian: A Course of Sermons on Evangelism in the Church Preached in the Chapel of Pusey House, Oxford*, 21–27. London: A. R. Mowbray, 1956.

"How Was Jesus Divine?" *Socratic Digest* 1 (June 1943): 24–25.

"Important Hypotheses Reconsidered, VIII. Typology." *Expository Times* 67 (May 1956): 228–31.

Interpretation and Belief. Edited by Charles C. Conti. London: SPCK, 1976.

Lord I Believe: Suggestions for Turning the Creed into Prayer. 2nd ed. London: SPCK, 1962.

Love Almighty and Ills Unlimited: An Essay on Providence and Evil, Containing the Nathaniel Taylor Lectures for 1961. Garden City, N.Y.: Doubleday, 1961.

"Mary, Scripture, and Tradition." In *The Blessed Virgin Mary: Essays by Anglican Writers*, edited by E. L. Mascall and H. S. Box, 27–52. London: Darton, Longman & Todd, 1963. Also in Farrer, *Interpretation and Belief*, 101–25.

"Meditation for Trinity Sunday." See "The Trinity in Whom We Live."

"Messianic Prophecy and Preparation for Christ." In *The Communication of the Gospel in New Testament Times: Some Recent Studies by Austin Farrer, C. F. Evans, J. A. Emerton, F. W. Beare, R. A. Markus, F. W. Dillistone*, 1–9. SPCK Theological Collections 2. London: SPCK, 1961. This sermon was preached before the University of Oxford in 1958.

"The Ministry in the New Testament." In *The Apostolic Ministry: Essays on the History and the Doctrine of Episcopacy*, edited by Kenneth E. Kirk, 113–82. London: Hodder & Stoughton, 1946.

"On Dispensing with Q." In *Studies in the Gospels: Essays in Memory of R. H. Lightfoot*, edited by D. E. Nineham, 55–88. Oxford: Basil Blackwell, 1957.

"On Looking below the Surface." *Proceedings of the Oxford Society of Historical Theology* (1959–60): 3–18. Reprinted in Farrer, *Interpretation and Belief,* 54–65; note references are to this reprinting.

"An Ordination Sermon." *Theology* 94 (May/June 1991): 166–67.

A Rebirth of Images: The Making of St. John's Apocalypse. Glasgow: University Press, 1949; Albany: State University of New York Press, 1986.

Reflective Faith: Essays in Philosophical Theology. Edited by Charles C. Conti. London: SPCK, 1972; Grand Rapids, Mich.: William B. Eerdmans, 1974.

"A Return to New Testament Christological Categories." *Theology* 26 (June 1933): 304–18.

The Revelation of St. John the Divine: Commentary on the English Text. Oxford: Clarendon Press, 1964.

"Review of *The Life of Jesus* by Maurice Goguel." *Theology* 27 (October1933): 229–30.

Said or Sung: An Arrangement of Homily and Verse. London: Faith Press, 1960.

Saving Belief: A Discussion of Essentials. London: Hodder and Stoughton, 1964. First American edition published in 1965 by Morehouse-Barlow in New York. Notes reference the 1964/1965 editions unless otherwise noted.

Saving Belief: A Discussion of Essentials. Edited by Susan Howatch. London: Mowbray and Morehouse, 1994. Pagination differs between the 1964/1965 and 1994 editions of this work. Notes give the page references to the Howatch edition parenthetically.

A Science of God? London: Geoffrey Bles, 1966. Published in the United States as *God Is Not Dead.*

St Matthew and St Mark. 2nd ed. London: Dacre Press, 1966.

A Study in St Mark. London: Dacre Press, 1951.

"The Theology of Morals." *Theology* 38 (May 1939): 332–41. Reprinted in Farrer, *Interpretation and Belief,* 176–85.

"Transcendence." Radio address. Recorded June 29, 1967, and transmitted on the BBC on August 8, 1967. Recording Number TLN26/RG033D. Typescript available in the Keble College Library Archives. Used by the kind permission of the Warden and Fellows of Keble College, Oxford, and the Trustees of K. D. Farrer. An edited version of this typescript appears as "Transcendence and 'Radical Theology'" in Farrer, *Reflective Faith.*

"The Trinity in Whom We Live." *Theology* 56 (September 1953): 322–27. Originally a radio address, "Meditation for Trinity Sunday," recorded on June 6, 1952 and transmitted on the BBC on June 8, 1952. Recording Number SLO 10356.

The Triple Victory: Christ's Temptations according to Saint Matthew. London: Faith Press; New York: Morehouse-Barlow, 1965. The archbishop of Canterbury's Lent book.

"Whereinsoever Any Is Bold, I Am [Sexagesima]." In *Bible Sermons: A Course Preached in the Chapel of Pusey House, Oxford,* by Christopher Evans and Austin Farrer, 32–38. London: A. R. Mowbray, 1963.

Words for Life. Edited by Charles Conti and Leslie Houlden. London: SPCK, 1993.

Other Works

"An Annotated Selection of the Works of Austin Farrer." In *Jacob's Ladder: Theology and Spirituality in the Thought of Austin Farrer,* by Charles Hefling, 127–32. Cambridge, Mass.: Cowley Publications, 1979.

Aquinas, Thomas. *Summa Theologica.* Translated by Fathers of the English Dominican Province. 5 vols. Westminster, Md.: Christian Classics, 1981.

Augustine, Saint. *Confessions.* Translated by Henry Chadwick. Oxford: Oxford University Press, 1991.

Barrett, C. K. "Review of *St Matthew and St Mark* by Austin Farrer." *Journal of Theological Studies,* n.s., 7 (1956): 107–10.

"Bibliography of Writings about Austin Farrer and Other Research Aids." In *Captured by the Crucified: The Practical Theology of Austin Farrer,* edited by David Hein and Edward Hugh Henderson, 197–208. New York: T. & T. Clark, 2004.

Blake, William. *Jerusalem.* In *The Poetry and Prose of William Blake.* Edited by David V. Erdman. Garden City, N.Y.: Doubleday, 1965.

The Book of Common Prayer, and Administration of the Sacraments and Other Rites and Ceremonies of the Church, Together with the Psalter or Psalms of David, according to the Use of the Episcopal Church. New York: Oxford University Press, 1990.

Booty, John. "An Elizabethan Addresses Modern Anglicanism: Richard Hooker and Theological Issues at the End of the Twentieth Century." *Anglican Theological Review* 71, no. 1 (1989): 8–24.

———. "Richard Hooker." In *The Spirit of Anglicanism,* edited by William J. Wolf, 1–45. Wilton, Conn.: Morehouse-Barlow, 1979.

Bruce, F. F., ed. *Promise and Fulfilment: Essays Presented to Professor S. H. Hooke, in Celebration of His Ninetieth Birthday, 21st January 1964, by Members of the Society for Old Testament Study and Others.* Edinburgh: T. & T. Clark, 1963.

Buber, Martin. *I and Thou.* 2nd ed. Translated by Ronald Gregor Smith. New York: Charles Scribner's Sons, 1958.

Bultmann, Rudolf. *The Gospel of John: A Commentary.* Translated by G. R. Beasley-Murray. General editors, R. W. N. Hoare and J. K. Riches. Philadelphia: Westminster Press, 1971.

"Chronological List of Published Writings by Austin Farrer 1933–76." In *A Hawk among Sparrows: A Biography of Austin Farrer,* by Philip Curtis, 250–57. London: SPCK, 1985.

Conti, Charles C. "A Chronological List of Austin M. Farrer's Published Writings, 1933–1981." In *For God and Clarity: New Essays in Honor of Austin Farrer,* edited by Jeffrey C. Eaton and Ann Loades, 191–200. Allison Park, Pa.: Pickwick Publications, 1983.

———. "Chronological List of Published Writings: 1933–1973." In *Reflective Faith: Essays in Philosophical Theology,* by Austin Farrer, 227–34. London: SPCK, 1972; Grand Rapids, Mich.: William B. Eerdmans, 1974.

———. "Editor's Preface." In *Reflective Faith: Essays in Philosophical Theology,* by Austin Farrer, viii–ix. London: SPCK, 1972; Grand Rapids, Mich.: William B. Eerdmans, 1974.

———. Preface to *Words for Life,* by Austin Farrer, vii–ix. London: SPCK, 1993.

Cooper, Robert M. "This Body of Hope." In *A Heart for the Future: Writings on the Christian Hope,* edited by Robert Boak Slocum, 31–47. New York: Church Publishing, 2004.

Crombie, I. M. "Farrer, Austin Marsden (1904–1968)." In *The Dictionary of National Biography, 1961–1970,* edited by E. T. Williams and C. S. Nicholls, 349–51. Oxford: Oxford University Press, 1981.

Curtis, Philip. *A Hawk among Sparrows: A Biography of Austin Farrer.* London: SPCK, 1985.

———. "The Rational Theology of Doctor Farrer." *Theology* 73 (June 1970): 249–56.

Cyril of Jerusalem. "Sermon I, The Prebaptismal Rites." In *The Awe-Inspiring Rites of Initiation: Baptismal Homilies of the Fourth Century,* by Edward Yarnold, S.J., 68–73, Middlegreen, Slough [U.K.]: St. Paul Publications, 1971.

Dalferth, Ingolf. "The Stuff of Revelation: Austin Farrer's Doctrine of Inspired Images." In *Hermeneutics, the Bible and Literary Criticism,* edited by Ann Loades, and Michael McLain, 71–95. New York: St. Martin's Press, 1992.

DuBose, William Porcher. "Christian Defense." In *Unity in the Faith,* edited by W. Norman Pittenger, 219–43. Greenwich, Conn.: Seabury Press, 1957. This essay originally appeared as "Christian Defense, or Apologetics," in *The Sunday School Teacher's Manual,* ed. William M. Groton, 2nd ed., pt. 3, 53–76 (Philadelphia: George W. Jacobs, 1911).

———. *The Ecumenical Councils.* 2nd ed. Vol. 3 of *Ten Epochs of Church History,* edited by John Fulton. Edinburgh: T. & T. Clark, 1897.

———. *The Reason of Life.* New York: Longmans, Green, 1911.

———. *Turning Points in My Life.* New York: Longmans, Green, 1912.

———. *Unity in the Faith.* Edited by W. Norman Pittenger. Greenwich, Conn.: Seabury Press, 1957.

Du Priest, Travis. "Spirit: Inner Witness and Guardian of the Soul." In *Engaging the Spirit: Essays on the Life and Theology of the Holy Spirit,* edited by Robert Boak Slocum, 17–31. New York: Church Publishing, 2001.

Eaton, Jeffrey C., and Ann Loades, eds. *For God and Clarity: New Essays in Honor of Austin Farrer.* Allison Park, Pa.: Pickwick Publications, 1983.

Edwards, Richard A. *Matthew's Narrative Portrait of Disciples: How the Text-Connoted Reader Is Informed.* Harrisburg, Pa.: Trinity Press International, 1997.

Eliot, T. S. "The Dry Salvages." In *Four Quartets,* 35–45. San Diego: Harvest/HBJ Books, 1988.

Elliott, Charlotte. "Just as I Am, without One Plea." In *The Hymnal 1982,* 693. New York: Church Hymnal Corporation, 1982.

Emmet, Dorothy M. *The Nature of Metaphysical Thinking.* London: Macmillan, 1949.

Farrer, Katharine. *At Odds with Morning.* London: Hodder & Stoughton, 1960.

———. *The Cretan Counterfeit.* London: Collins, 1954. First American edition, Boulder, Colo.: Rue Morgue Press, 2004.

———. *Gownsman's Gallows.* London: Hodder & Stoughton, 1957. First American edition, Boulder, Colo.: Rue Morgue Press, 2005.

———. *The Missing Link.* London: Collins, 1952. First American edition, Boulder, Colo.: Rue Morgue Press, 2004.

Forsman, Rodger. "Revelation and Understanding: A Defence of Tradition." In *Hermeneutics, the Bible and Literary Criticism,* edited by Ann Loades, and Michael McLain, 46–68. New York: St. Martin's Press, 1992.

Gardner, Helen. *The Business of Criticism.* Oxford: Clarendon Press, 1959.

———. *In Defence of the Imagination.* Cambridge: Harvard University Press, 1982.

———. *The Limits of Literary Criticism: Reflections on the Interpretation of Poetry and Scripture.* London: Oxford University Press, 1956.

Gill, Jerry H. "Divine Action as Mediated." *Harvard Theological Review* 80, no. 3 (1987): 369–78.

Golitzin, Hieromonk Alexander. "'I See Your Bridal Chamber Adorned,' an Eastern Orthodox Reflection on the Eschaton in Light of the 'Pattern' of Divine Worship." In *A Heart for the Future: Writings on the Christian Hope,* edited by Robert Boak Slocum, 82–95. New York: Church Publishing, 2004.

Groton, William M., ed. *The Sunday School Teacher's Manual.* 2nd ed. Philadelphia: G. W. Jacobs, 1911.

Harries, Richard. "Celebration of the Centenary of the Birth of Austin Farrer, October 11th, 2004." *Diocese of Oxford,* September 23, 2004. http://www.oxford.anglican .org/. Sermon preached by the bishop of Oxford at Oriel College, Oxford, September 8, 2004.

———. "'We Know on Our Knees . . .': Intellectual, Imaginative and Spiritual Unity in the Theology of Austin Farrer." In *Divine Action: Studies Inspired by the Philosophical Theology of Austin Farrer,* edited by Brian Hebblethwaite and Edward Henderson, 21–33. Edinburgh: T. & T. Clark, 1990.

Hebblethwaite, Brian. "Austin Farrer's Concept of Divine Providence." *Theology* 73 (December 1970): 541–51.

Hebblethwaite, Brian, and Edward Henderson, eds. *Divine Action: Studies Inspired by the Philosophical Theology of Austin Farrer.* Edinburgh: T. & T. Clark, 1990.

Hebert, A. G., ed. *The Parish Communion: A Book of Essays.* London: Society for Promoting Christian Knowledge and Macmillan, 1937.

Hefling, Charles. "Farrer's Scriptural Divinity." In *Captured by the Crucified: The Practical Theology of Austin Farrer,* edited by David Hein and Edward Hugh Henderson, 149–72. New York: T. & T. Clark, 2004.

———. *Jacob's Ladder: Theology and Spirituality in the Thought of Austin Farrer.* Cambridge, Mass.: Cowley Publications, 1979.

Hein, David, and Edward Hugh Henderson, eds. *Captured by the Crucified: The Practical Theology of Austin Farrer.* New York: T. & T. Clark, 2004.

Henderson, Edward Hugh. "The God Who Undertakes Us." In *Captured by the Crucified: The Practical Theology of Austin Farrer,* edited by David Hein and Edward Hugh Henderson, 66–99. New York: T. & T. Clark, 2004.

Hick, John. Foreword to *Reflective Faith: Essays in Philosophical Theology,* by Austin Farrer, xiii–xv. London: SPCK, 1972; Grand Rapids, Mich.: William B. Eerdmans, 1974.

Hooker, Richard. *The Folger Library Edition of the Works of Richard Hooker.* Vol. 2, *Of the Laws of Ecclesiastical Polity,* edited by W. Speed Hill. Cambridge: Belknap Press of Harvard University Press, 1977.

Hooper, Walter. *C. S. Lewis: A Companion & Guide.* London: Fount; San Francisco: HarperSanFrancisco, 1996.

Howatch, Susan. *Absolute Truths.* New York: Alfred A. Knopf, 1995.

———. Introduction to *Saving Belief: A Discussion of Essentials,* by Austin Farrer, vii–xi. London: Mowbray and Morehouse, 1994.

The Hymnal 1982. New York: Church Hymnal Corporation, 1982.

"In Memoriam, Dr. Austin Farrer." *Church Times* (London), January 3, 1969, 15.

Jasper, David. *Coleridge as Poet and Religious Thinker.* Allison Park, Pa.: Pickwick Publications, 1985.

Jones, Alan. "The Crack in the Heart." In *A New Conversation: Essays on the Future of Theology and the Episcopal Church,* edited by Robert B. Slocum, 109–19. New York: Church Publishing, 1999. 109–19.

Jung, Carl G. "Foreword to the Fourth (Swiss) Edition (September, 1950)." In Jung, *Symbols of Transformation,* xxiii–xxvi.

———. "Foreword to the Second (German) Edition (November, 1924)." In Jung, *Symbols of Transformation,* xxviii–xxix.

———. "Foreword to the Third (German) Edition (November, 1937)." In Jung, *Symbols of Transformation,* xxvii.

———. *Man and His Symbols.* Garden City, N.Y.: Doubleday, 1964.

———. *Symbols of Transformation: An Analysis of the Prelude to a Case of Schizophrenia.* 2nd ed. Translated by R. F. C. Hull. Vol. 5 of *The Collected Works of C. G. Jung.* Princeton, N. J.: Princeton University Press, 1967.

Kermode, Frank. *The Genesis of Secrecy: On the Interpretation of Narrative.* The Charles Eliot Norton Lectures, 1977–78. Cambridge, Mass. and London: Harvard University Press, 1979.

King, Martin Luther, Jr. "The Answer to a Perplexing Question." In *Strength to Love,* 127–36. Philadelphia: Fortress Press, 1981.

Kirk, Kenneth E., ed. *The Apostolic Ministry: Essays on the History and the Doctrine of Episcopacy.* London: Hodder & Stoughton, 1946.

Leibniz, G. W. *Theodicy: Essays on the Goodness of God, the Freedom of Man, and the Origin of Evil.* Edited, with an introduction by Austin Farrer. Translated by E. M.

Huggard from C. J. Gerhardt's edition of the *Collected Philosophical Works, 1875–1990*. LaSalle, Ill.: Open Court, 1985.

Lewis, C. S. *A Grief Observed*. London and Boston: Faber and Faber, 1961.

———. Preface to *A Faith of Our Own*, by Austin Farrer, 7–10. Cleveland: World Publishing, 1960.

Lewis, H. D. *Our Experience of God*. London: George Allen & Unwin and Macmillan, 1959.

Loades, Ann. "Austin Farrer on Love Almighty." In *For God and Clarity: New Essays in Honor of Austin Farrer*, edited by Jeffrey C. Eaton and Ann Loades, 93–107. Allison Park, Pa.: Pickwick Publications, 1983.

———. "The Vitality of Tradition: Austin Farrer and Friends." In *Captured by the Crucified: The Practical Theology of Austin Farrer*, edited by David Hein and Edward Hugh Henderson, 15–46. New York: T. & T. Clark, 2004.

Loades, Ann, and Michael McLain, eds. *Hermeneutics, the Bible and Literary Criticism*. New York: St. Martin's Press, 1992.

Luther, Martin. *The Bondage of the Will*. Translated by Philip S. Watson in collaboration with Benjamin Drewery. In *Luther's Works*, vol. 33, edited by Philip S. Watson, gen. ed. Helmut T. Lehmann. Philadelphia: Fortress Press, 1972.

Mack, Daphne. "'Greatest Anglican Mind of 20th Century' Is Conference Focus." *Episcopal News Service*, October 26, 2004. http://www.episcopalchurch.org/3577_53360_ENG_HTM.htm (accessed June 10, 2006).

Macmurray, John. *A Challenge to the Churches, Religion and Democracy*. London: Kegan Paul, Trench, Trubner, 1941.

———. *Persons in Relation*. Atlantic Highlands, N.J. and London: Humanities Press, 1991.

Macquarrie, John. *Christology Revisited*. Harrisburg, Pa.: Trinity Press International, 1998.

———. *Jesus Christ in Modern Thought*. London: SCM Press; Philadelphia: Trinity Press International, 1990.

Marcel, Gabriel. *Being and Having*. Translated by Katharine Farrer. Westminster: Dacre Press, 1949.

Mascall, E. L., and H. S. Box, eds. *The Blessed Virgin Mary: Essays by Anglican Writers*. London: Darton, Longman & Todd, 1963.

McGrath, Alister E., ed. *The Christian Theology Reader*. 2nd ed. Oxford: Blackwell, 2001.

McLain, F. Michael, and W. Mark Richardson, eds. *Human and Divine Agency: Anglican, Catholic, and Lutheran Perspectives*. Lanham, Md.: University Press of America, 1999.

Mitchell, Basil, ed. *Faith and Logic: Oxford Essays in Philosophical Theology*. London: George Allen & Unwin, 1957.

Murray, J. O. F. *DuBose as a Prophet of Unity*. London: Society for Promoting Christian Knowledge, 1924.

Nineham, D. E., ed. *Studies in the Gospels: Essays in Memory of R. H. Lightfoot.* Oxford: Basil Blackwell, 1957.

Oliver, Simon. "The Theodicy of Austin Farrer." *Heythrop Journal* 39, no. 3 (1988): 280–97.

Peterson, Jeffrey. "A Pioneer Narrative Critic and His Synoptic Hypothesis: Austin Farrer and Gospel Interpretation." *Society of Biblical Literature 2000 Seminar Papers* 39 (2000): 651–72.

Platten, Stephen. "Diaphanous Thought: Spirituality and Theology in the Work of Austin Farrer." *Anglican Theological Review* 69, no. 1 (1987): 30–50.

Price, Francis Douglas. "Speech at Keble London Dinner." January 7, 1969. Unpublished manuscript available in Keble College Archive. Used by the kind permission of the Warden and Fellows of Keble College, Oxford.

Rhoads, David. Preface to *Mark as Story: An Introduction to the Narrative of a Gospel,* by David Rhoads and Donald Michie, xv–xvi. Philadelphia: Fortress Press, 1982.

Rhoads, David, and Donald Michie. *Mark as Story: An Introduction to the Narrative of a Gospel.* Philadelphia: Fortress Press, 1982.

Richardson, W. Mark. "A Look at Austin Farrer's Theory of Agency." In *Human and Divine Agency: Anglican, Catholic, and Lutheran Perspectives,* edited by F. Michael McLain and W. Mark Richardson, 121–48. Lanham, Md.: University Press of America, 1999.

Sayers, Dorothy L. *The Mind of the Maker.* New York: Harcourt, Brace, 1941.

Slocum, Robert Boak. "An Answering Heart: Reflections on Saving Participation." *Anglican Theological Review* 84, no. 4 (2002): 1009–15.

———, ed. *Engaging the Spirit: Essays on the Life and Theology of the Holy Spirit.* New York: Church Publishing, 2001.

———. "Farrer in the Pulpit: A Systematic Introduction to His Sermons." *Anglican Theological Review* 86, no. 3 (2004): 493–503.

———. "A Heart for the Future: Reflections on the Christian Hope." In *A Heart for the Future: Writings on the Christian Hope,* edited by Robert Boak Slocum, 1–30. New York: Church Publishing, 2004.

———, ed. *A Heart for the Future: Writings on the Christian Hope.* New York: Church Publishing, 2004.

———. "Kingdom Come: Preliminaries for a Relational Theology of Hope." *Anglican Theological Review* 82, no. 3 (2000): 571–78.

———. "Light in a Burning-Glass: The Theological Witness of Austin Farrer." *Anglican Theological Review* 85, no. 2 (2003): 365–73.

———, ed. *A New Conversation: Essays on the Future of Theology and the Episcopal Church.* New York: Church Publishing, 1999.

———, ed. *Prophet of Justice, Prophet of Life: Essays on William Stringfellow.* New York: Church Publishing, 1997.

———. "Romantic Religion and the Witness of James DeKoven." In *To Hear Celestial Harmonies: Essays on the Witness of James DeKoven and the DeKoven Center,* edited by Robert Boak Slocum and Travis Talmadge Du Priest, 15–32. Cincinnati: Forward Movement, 2002.

———. *The Theology of William Porcher DuBose: Life, Movement, and Being.* Columbia: University of South Carolina Press, 2000.

———. "William Stringfellow and the Christian Witness against Death." In *Prophet of Justice, Prophet of Life: Essays on William Stringfellow,* edited by Robert Boak Slocum, 18–39. New York: Church Publishing, 1997.

Stocker, Margarita. "God in Theory: Milton, Literature and Theodicy." *Journal of Literature & Theology* 1 (March 1987): 70–88.

Stringfellow, William. *An Ethic for Christians and Other Aliens in a Strange Land.* Waco, Texas: Word Books, 1973.

Thomas, Owen C., ed. *God's Activity in the World: The Contemporary Problem.* American Academy of Religion Studies in Religion, no. 31. Chico, Calif.: Scholars Press, 1983.

Wilson, A. N. *C. S. Lewis: A Biography.* London: Collins; New York: Norton, 1990.

Wilson, M. P. "St. John, the Trinity, and the Language of the Spirit." *Scottish Journal of Theology* 41 (December 1988): 471–83.

Yarnold, Edward, S.J. *The Awe-Inspiring Rites of Initiation: Baptismal Homilies of the Fourth Century.* Middlegreen, Slough [U.K.]: St. Paul Publications, 1971.

Index